AF660043

VEER MUNSHI

THE DIALOGUES SERIES

Ranjit Hoskote and Nancy Adajania

VEER MUNSHI

foundation b & g

Popular Prakashan
www.popularprakashan.com

Popular Prakashan Pvt Ltd
301, Mahalaxmi Chambers
22, Bhulabhai Desai Road
Mumbai 400026
www.popularprakashan.com

© foundation b & g

First Published 2011

All rights reserved

ISBN 978-81-7991-638-4
(4386)

Printed by
Saurabh Printers Pvt. Ltd.

Published by Harsha Bhatkal for
Popular Prakashan Pvt. Ltd. and
foundation b & g
301, Mahalaxmi Chambers
22, Bhulabhai Desai Road
Mumbai 400026

Special thanks
Neelima Acharya
Smeeta Bhatkal
Rumki Fernandes
Anant Gawande
Vinayak Gawande
Mahendra Ghanekar
Vasuki Sundaram

Contents

The Dialogues Series : An Introduction

foundation b & g is a contemporary arts publishing and curatorial initiative, launched in January 2009 by Popular Prakashan, an 87-year-old publishing house that pioneered high-quality publishing in the social sciences, history and literature in India. The Foundation aims to develop a serious knowledge infrastructure for India's contemporary visual arts. Its mission is to inform the enthusiast and to augment the bandwidth of the informed. The Foundation's objective is to achieve a convergence among artists, critics, curators, viewers and readers. It has planned a publishing programme that includes entry-level, intermediate and specialist books. At school level, it will model an art pedagogy that is responsive and participatory: to cultivate new generations that will not regard culture as alien to normal life, but will embrace it as a necessary condition of being.

foundation b & g, which already has seven exhibitions and three monographs to its credit, now presents an important publishing initiative, The Dialogues Series, which is targeted to art enthusiasts in general and students of art in particular.

The Dialogues Series explores the concerns, careers and contexts of some of India's most acclaimed artists. Those featured in this continuing series of books include Anju Dodiya, Ashim Purkayastha, Atul Dodiya, Baiju Parthan, Gargi Raina, Iranna G R, Madhvi Parekh, Manu Parekh, Jagannath Panda, Justin Ponmany, Ranbir Kaleka, Riyas Komu, Sumedh Rajendran and Veer Munshi. They represent several generations and positions within the richly diverse domain of contemporary Indian art.

Each book in The Dialogues Series engages with an individual artist. It takes the form of an extended conversation between the artist and the authors, Ranjit Hoskote and Nancy Adajania, two of India's best known and most authoritative critics.

These books are not intended to be mere interviews, but will create an understanding of the artists' work at different levels. As the authors themselves put it, "The Dialogues Series performs three functions. First, it provides sharply etched portraits of the artists and critically engaged accounts of their work. We see each artist's journey in review, with its distinctive transitions, breakthroughs and evolutionary rhythms. Second, it situates the imagination and lifeworld of the artists within larger art-historical genealogies, cultural narratives and political discussions, both Indian and global. And third, this series aims to create a discursive space in which both enthusiasts and scholars can reflect on the arguments that art and criticism conduct with history. We believe that the history of art does not simply revolve around the personalities of individual artists or the trends of the day; it also records the vital historical and philosophical questions that are posed and played out on the contested terrain of art."

A note on the methodology of The Dialogues Series would be relevant. These conversations have unfolded over space and time, across sites in India and overseas: the artists and the authors have travelled together, sharing thoughts, views, anecdotes and arguments. They have continued these exchanges over email, chat, telephone and Skype. The participants have gone away, reflected on their exchanges, researched their positions, and met again. What The Dialogues Series presents, therefore, is not simple transcripts, but compositions that have been crafted, textured and woven into their present shape.

Importantly, these are not interviews, but dialogues among fellow stake-holders. The authors are long-time participants in the Indian art world and contributors to its development since the late 1980s (Hoskote) and the mid-1990s (Adajania). As such, they share a unique proximity with their interlocutors: as friends, colleagues and collaborators in the making of the vibrant globalisation-era Indian art scene. Together, the artists and the authors draw out the oral histories, the untold narratives of this scene. Through The Dialogue Series, many of the accepted notions of Indian art history are re-evaluated and new, surprising discoveries are made. The artists and the authors pose questions to one another, not only to draw out answers, but also to re-draw the contemporary cultural debate.

Each book in The Dialogues Series also offers its readers a concise biographical text about the artist and a set of 16 images of key works from her or his oeuvre.

On behalf of foundation b & g, I would like to thank Nancy and Ranjit not only for authoring this series, which we hope will become an important source book for students of contemporary Indian art, but also for their active participation and involvement in all the activities of the Foundation. This is but the first important step taken by the Foundation in moving towards a greater role in the documentation of subjects related to visual art in the Indian context, more particularly in a format that is accessible and affordable.

Harsha Bhatkal
Chairman
foundation b & g

Artist Biography

VEER MUNSHI (born 1955) earned a BA from Kashmir University, Srinagar (1975) and a BFA in Painting from the M. S. University, Baroda (1981). He has held 14 solo exhibitions during the last 16 years with, among others, Art Heritage (New Delhi, 1992); Gallery Burswood (Perth, 1996); E. C. Galleria (Edinburgh, 1997); Gallery Espace (New Delhi, 2003); Tao Art Gallery (Mumbai, 2004); Art Alive (India Habitat Centre, New Delhi, 2006); AIFACS Gallery (New Delhi, 1995); Jehangir Art Gallery (Mumbai, 1995 and 2004); and at the United Nations (Geneva, 1996). Munshi's most recent solo exhibition, 'Shrapnel', was curated by Ranjit Hoskote and produced by foundation b & g (Tao Art Gallery, Mumbai and the Birla Academy of Art & Culture, Kolkata, 2009–2010).

Munshi has participated in numerous curated and group exhibitions. Among these are 'A Gift for Gandhi' (SAHMAT, New Delhi and Mumbai/1995); 'Ways of Resistance' (SAHMAT, New Delhi/2002); 'Art on the Move', curated by Vivan Sundaram (SAHMAT, New Delhi/2002); the 11th Asian Art Biennale (Dhaka/2004); 'Identity Alienation Amity', curated by Bina Sarkar (Tao Art Gallery, Mumbai/2005); *Tehelka*'s 'Art for Freedom' (London/2008); the World Social Forum, Karachi/2006; the India Art Summit, New Delhi/2008; 'Image, Music and Text', curated by Ram Rahman (SAHMAT, New Delhi/2009); and 'ZIP Files', edited by Ranjit Hoskote (foundation b & g, Mumbai and New Delhi/2009). Munshi's art is informed by his extensive and engaged travels as artist, cultural organiser and cultural activist. He has visited Cambodia, China, Egypt, Greece, Italy, Jordan, Kenya, Morocco,

Mexico, Pakistan, Singapore, South Africa, Switzerland, Thailand, Turkey, and the UK. Fayaz 'Gashtaruq' made a documentary for Doordarshan Television on Munshi's art in 2002; K. Bikram Singh made a documentary on his work in 2003. Munshi lives and works in Gurgaon.

1

The Dead Sea

Jordan (17/01/2009)

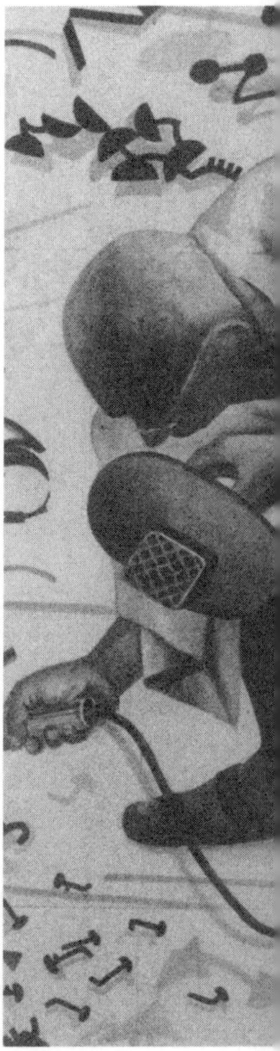

The Dead Sea
Jordan

Ranjit Hoskote: Veer, it's a pleasure to welcome you to the Dead Sea Studios of foundation b & g! We've spent these last few days travelling together across Jordan, absorbing the persistence and synthesis of the Hellenic, Roman, Jewish, and Arab cultures in this region. But we've also encountered various deeply moving testimonies to the harrowing religious warfare staged in West Asia, with the imprint of the Crusades still present in castles and museums, and the consequences of the Israeli-Arab conflict written across the geography. Nancy and I would like to begin this conversation by asking you a few questions about your art practice, which has, in recent times, returned repeatedly to the themes of war and the setting of the conflict zone.

Nancy Adajania: In your paintings and sculpture installations, you have addressed the precariousness of being an artist in a situation where normality has been disrupted by political forces. In fact, a situation where disruption has become the prevailing normality. Has your own predicament of being Kashmiri in the early 21st century contributed to this tendency in your art? Naturally, we realise that you would not wish to be limited by the label of 'Kashmiri artist'. But could you tell us about the historical and personal events that led you to your current artistic concerns?

Veer Munshi: Yes, definitely. All things changed for me in 1990. When I lost my address, it was as if I was born again with an identity crisis. That date had a very definite impact on my art practice too.

Born and brought up in Srinagar, I took a BA from S. P. College, Kashmir University, in 1976. I then went to M. S. University, Baroda, to study fine arts. On completing my BFA there in 1981, I returned purposefully to Kashmir to settle down. I was not very ambitious in a professional sense, and just wanted to get down to my art practice back there. But everything changed with the rise of militancy in Kashmir during the late 1980s, the killing of liberal and creative figures, and the targeting of the Pandit minority. This was a challenge to the secular values and composite culture of Kashmir. My belief in Kashmiri Muslims as peace-loving and progressive people remains strong. My memory is still fresh, of going with Shabbir, Shora Bashir, Suraj Tiku, and Aftab Ahmed on adventures—boating, trekking, with our watercolour pads, wandering in search of fresh spots to paint. I continue to share the same bond with them. We are an extension of each other, speak the same language, and share a common cultural ethos. And yet, with the exodus of the Kashmiri Pandits from the Valley in the early 1990s, a moderate, educated community with secular values was pushed out. Whose purpose did it serve? Maybe it served the agenda of Islamist, separatist, and fundamentalist forces. Even so, I would never believe that such forces can last long in a land that has such a strong history of Sufi saints and Rishis.

NA: Did you leave Kashmir during the mass exodus of Kashmiri Pandits that began in January 1990?

VM: I remember the exact date and time. It was 5 am on the morning of 4 February 1990. I was the first of my family to move out. I had to move out because some of the individuals, who were active in political militancy, and even the separatist movement, were friends of my friends, people with whom we had a dialogue. But when the militancy grew in intensity, our dialogue took a different turn. It became suffocating, there was a feeling of being choked, and our freedom of expression got sealed off. Some of these individuals asked me to help them with posters and propaganda images. This

I could not do. So my position became difficult, and I had to leave the Valley. I went to Shimla first but didn't feel at home there, so I went to Delhi. The mass exodus of Kashmiri Pandits began on the night of 19 January 1990. All that day and into the night, threatening slogans were playing over the loudspeakers.

RH: Yes, I recall those slogans well. They were intended to terrorise the Hindu minority. '*Kashmir mein agar rehna hai, Allah-o-Akbar kehna hai!*' (If you want to live in Kashmir, learn to say 'Allah-o-Akbar!') and '*Yahan kya chalega, Nizam-e-Mustafa!*' (It's going to come, the Kingdom of the Prophet!).

VM: All this created the threat perception that we were in a minority, and we realised forcefully that we were the minority. Within a couple of months, most Kashmiri Pandits left the Valley. Soon after I moved out, I heard that the rest of my family had also moved out. I went back to Jammu to search for my parents, to find out where they were.

NA: And so the Kashmiri Pandits became refugees in their own country. Where did your parents move to, in Jammu?

VM: They had rented a room in Jammu. When I went to visit them, the landlord did not allow me to stay with them, saying guests were not allowed. After that, we dispersed in different directions. I went to Delhi. One of my brothers went to Himachal Pradesh; the other went to Hyderabad and took our parents to live with him. My father died early, in 1997. He had spent his last years in depression. My mother, who still longs to return to her homeland, has lived in Delhi ever since.

RH: How did you find your feet in Delhi?

VM: On arriving in Delhi, I stayed at the Lalit Kala Akademi's guesthouse, Bahawalpur House, in Mandi House Circle.

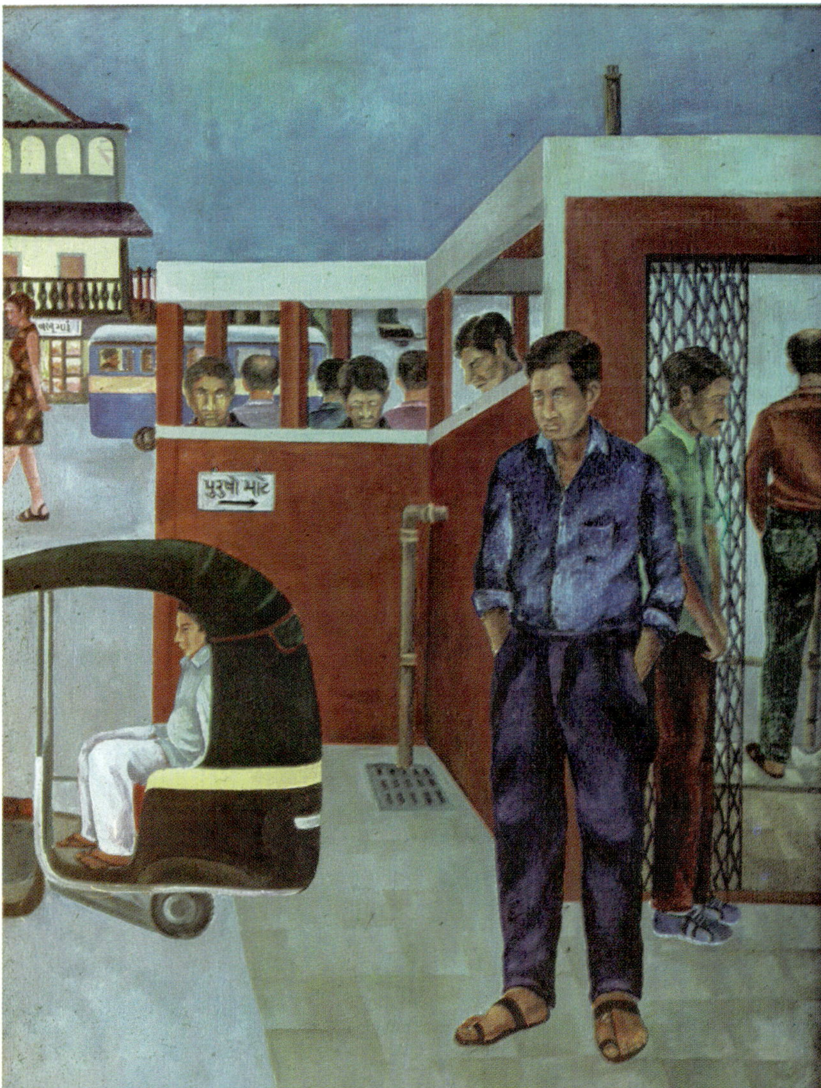

Purusho Maate (1981)
Oil on canvas

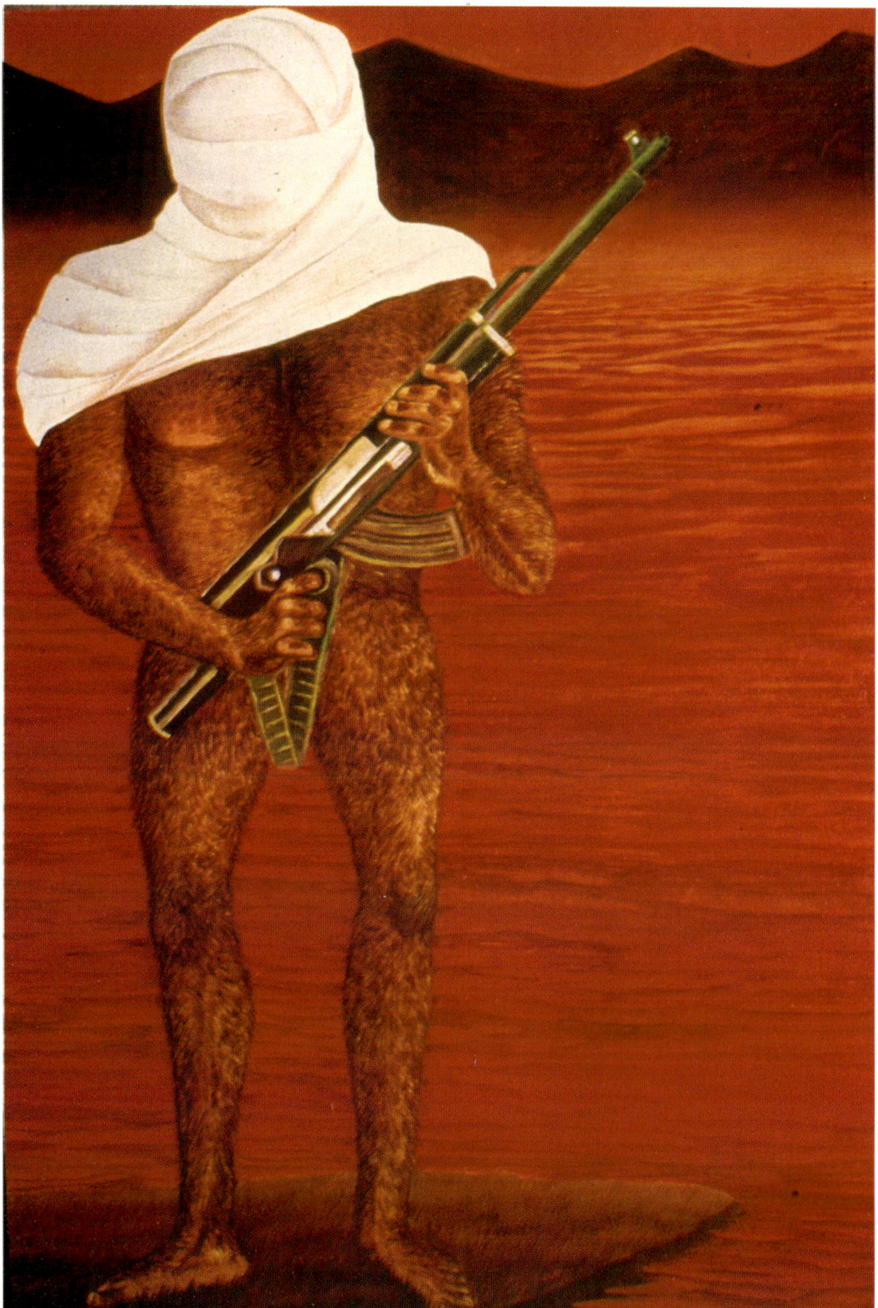

Terrorist On a Floating Land (1990)
Oil on canvas

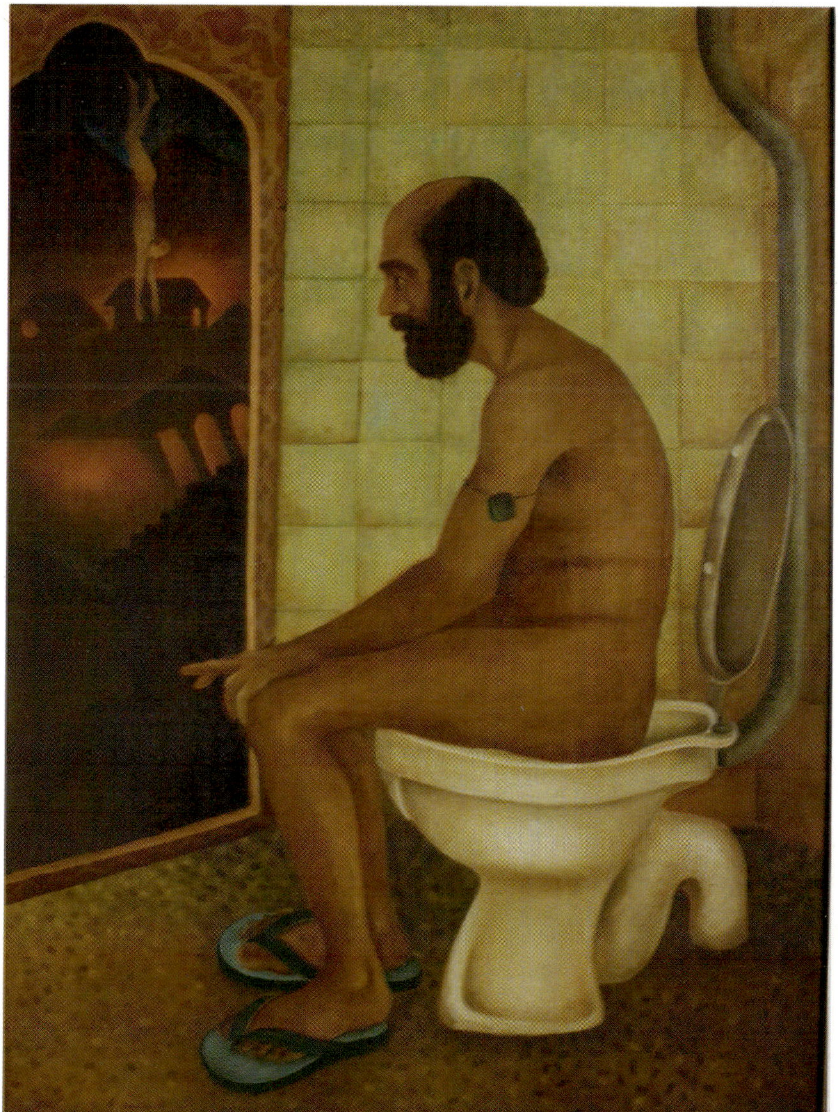

Self-Contemplation (1992)
Oil on canvas

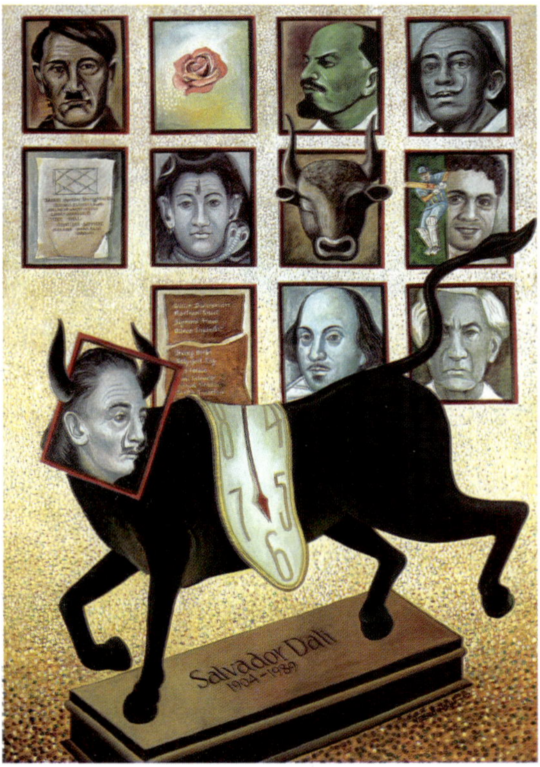

Taurian Gallery (2003)
Oil on canvas

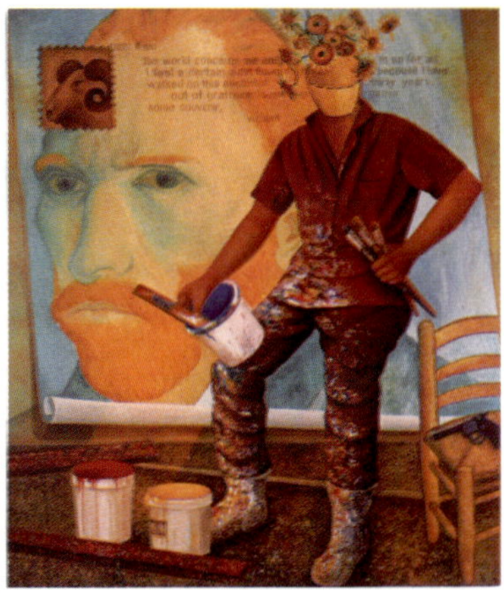

Impulsive Arian: Van Gogh (2003)
Oil on canvas

Bahawalpur House was a great place to be in those days. We were charged Rs 5 for a bed, and fellow artists such as Subodh Gupta, Sanjeev Sinha, Shambhavi, and many more were living there in those days. Kishen Kaw, Vijay Koul, and Satish Kar had come from Kashmir. But many of them could not sustain their practice. For the Kashmiris, it was not easy to come to Delhi as refugees and sustain themselves as art practitioners. The market was dicey. I stayed at Bahawalpur House for three or four months, looking for work, with a break of one day every week to honour the LKA guesthouse rules. That night was usually spent in a park nearby. Our support structure was a series of odd jobs. My first job got me Rs 40 a day, a daily wage job at the expo centre of Pragati Maidan. Painting was not in my mind then, because I was fighting to survive. Those years of struggle were the real beginning of our careers.

It was all about survival, how to earn a little and learn to live on it. But then, finally, one day, somebody wanted a painting from me. I said I didn't even have money for the materials, so they gave me an advance. I still remember it was about Rs 1,500. That day, I ate good food, a meat dish, at the Gomati Guest House in Bengali Market. (*Peals of laughter*) It was a long time since I had had nice food. In a couple of days, I was left with only Rs 300. Now I had to give the person a work. I bought the paint and bought a canvas, but Bahawalpur House was not conducive to paint in. There were many people and a lot of noise. So somebody suggested I go to the Garhi artists' studios. I went to Garhi, but no one would give me an inch of studio space there. They told me to go and join the graphics department. But I had to paint. There was the rest of the money that was coming, if I painted that picture. I knew I had to do it. So, I barged into the community workshop in Garhi. In the passage, there would be Dillu [Mrinalini Mukherjee], Manjit [Bawa] and Arpana [Caur], and many other artists inside, in their own studio cabins.

NA: Did you finish the painting?

VM: (*Laughs*) At that time, I thought I would make pretty landscapes for survival. But nothing of that kind came out of me. I struggled with myself, but could not do what I could have easily done earlier. I thought, let me do something new. That's when I made 'Terrorist On A Floating Land'. I began to see Kashmir as a floating land.

NA: So could we call this your breakthrough painting?

VM: It was my first painting on a political subject, dated 1990. It was a cathartic release after trauma. All the tensions that were building up inside me came to a dramatic head when I was working on that picture. I had read and heard about inspiration, but it was a myth to me. It was only while I was painting this picture that it turned into a reality for me. I thought, some miracle is happening, and I could not share it with anybody at that moment. For the first time, I believed in the strength of the language of painting. It was as if a super-spirit had given me therapy for my mental state of that period. It gave me the energy to continue to bear witness to what was happening, through a series of morbid images or different episodes that I captured. It was as if I was documenting the events that were unfolding rapidly in Kashmir. You will remember the kidnapping of K. Doraiswamy, executive director of the Indian Oil Corporation, by the militants. That came into my paintings. I painted 'Mukhbir', the informer. The paintings 'Tribute to Lassa Koul' and 'Tribute to Ghulam Mohammed' were for victims of the murder machine of the militancy. 'Hope against Hope', 'Satanic Call', 'Exiles of the Valley', 'Where Do the Strings Lead?', 'Moods of the Valley', and many other paintings evoke the different moments and feelings of the complex Kashmir situation of the early 1990s. But then, people said, 'What are you doing, do you want to die hungry? Nobody will buy these paintings'. I was not able to tell them why I was doing what I was doing. I didn't know whether it was good art or bad art, but I didn't care. The paintings did not sell, but I worked on. I thought I would go on painting like this, because it brought me psychological relief and creative release, and would find some other way of earning money.

RH: Was it around this time that you taught at a school for a while?

VM: It was 1991. I asked my colleagues in Garhi how I could survive by using my education in art. They said, 'Do a school job'. I asked if there was a good school I could apply to, and somebody suggested St. Columba's. Apparently they had a vacancy. I went to see the principal and said I wanted to teach. He asked if I had any experience. I said no, but I have confidence. My forefathers were Pandits, famous as teachers, I told him, so I would manage. He gave me a grin, took me to a class. I gave my first lecture, and got the job, at Rs 1,500 a month. Now the problem was the timing. The school started its day at 7 am. And I was not in the habit of getting up early. At the guesthouse, all kinds of artists would come by, and the evenings would go on until morning. To reach St. Columba's, I had to catch a 6 am bus from Bengali Market. I kept missing that bus. So one day, I decided to start sleeping in my daytime clothes, with my shoes on. So I could literally jump out of bed, brush my teeth, and run for the bus. I still missed it, often, and the principal would be amused. I worked at the school for one and a half years. It didn't work much for me.

RH: (*laughing*) After which, they decided to get somebody who could catch the bus and get to school on time. And you returned full time to the studio.

NA: But it was also around this time that you had your first show, with Alkazi, at Art Heritage in Delhi. What kind of reaction did you get from your viewers? At that time, the militancy in Kashmir was already peaking, but the issues were not well understood and one could say that they still remain unclear to many. How did people react to terrorism as a subject of serious paintings shown in a mainstream gallery?

VM: Yes, Alkazi gave me my first exhibition in 1992. He recognised something in my work, or perhaps he liked it. All the images of terror, horror, anguish, and disturbance went into my first show. That was the beginning of my public career as an artist. My show was much talked about. It initiated a great deal of debate with a cross section of people, including activists from the then newly formed SAHMAT [Safdar Hashmi Memorial Trust], to whom I was introduced for the first time. After some discussion, they realised that my art was a personal testimony to a crisis situation, and not Hindu right-wing propaganda. Once they understood this, they supported my art. Later, I began to participate in SAHMAT's exhibitions, beginning with 'Postcards for Gandhi' in 1995. I also had an encounter with the connoisseur and cultural activist Rajiv Sethi, who had the idealistic dream of taking the Pandits back to Kashmir. After a little while, he realised that it was not going to be easy. These meetings also gave me a sense of what Delhi is about, how it works. I continued to express my sense of crisis. In 1992, I created a tent installation, 'Root-Uproot', with Kishen Kaw and Sushil Pandit. It was a polythene tent. I was concerned about the exodus.

NA: And what kind of objects did the tent contain?

VM: The tent had artefacts and ritualistic objects, and some old photographs. It had some books, Sanskrit books, and things that came from our ancestors or referred to our property. We assembled things that I felt would suit the project. I was also attracted to the image of the boat as a metaphor of a society crossing stormy waters, carrying different characters, the faces of different people. Migration, partition, and division remained my main concerns, and they flowed into my 2006 exhibition, 'Encounter', produced by Art Alive at the India Habitat Centre, New Delhi. Migration as displacement for political or economic reasons, partition as the division of what had once been the same land, and division for religious, sectarian, or ideological reasons—these are the three broad areas that I am still working on. I have experienced these, and maybe I am meant to work on these areas. Sometimes I do other things, different stuff that is fairly good, but then I feel: This is not really me. I always question myself about whether I am doing something under pressure, for some reason of momentary importance, or whether I am doing something that is truly my interest.

RH: But you have explored a wide variety of concerns that are not related to Kashmir, or directly political in tenor. I would think of your zodiac series, for instance...

NA: ...which you showed in the form of two exhibitions with Gallery Espace, New Delhi. Who were the 12 characters that you chose, corresponding to each sign of the zodiac?

VM: My zodiac had nothing to do with astrology. It was a convenient structure through which I could come closer to characters about whom I knew, or had heard about, or whose works I had read or seen, or who had historical significance, whether positive or negative. I thought the framework of the 12 signs would allow me to restrict myself to a set of limited, manageable images. I started with the intention of making 12 works but ended up making around 40. These were shown 12 at a time, though. Pisces was represented by Bhupen Khakhar, Aries by Van Gogh and Charlie Chaplin. Taurus grew into what I titled 'The Taurian Gallery', with Dali, Bertrand Russell, Hitler, Satyajit Ray, Shakespeare, and Sachin Tendulkar. Gemini had Marilyn Monroe, Paul Gauguin, and I thought, why don't I put myself in here as well, after all, it's my birth sign! Under the sign of Cancer, I had Julius Caesar and Nelson Mandela. Under Leo, Bill Clinton. Virgo had M. F. Husain, Michael Jackson, and Mother Teresa. Libra was represented by Mahatma Gandhi, Scorpio by Pablo Picasso, and Sagittarius by Osho. Under Capricorn were Jesus, Jinnah, and Atal Bihari Vajpayee. And Charles Darwin represented Aquarius.

NA: Do you use the zodiac series as an occasion to research the lives and works of these figures who have produced our historical present?

VM: Yes. The zodiac series gave me the chance to investigate and research their work more closely. It is so interesting to trace a set of references, one thing leads to another. Nancy, in another conversation that we have had elsewhere, you once asked me why I return to the human face as a focus. I draw faces because, when I draw another person and feel what it is like to live inside his or her skin, I stretch my abilities to their furthest and I also expand my experience with the experience of the other person.

RH: Your zodiac is a private pantheon, isn't it? And it gave you some relief from the unremitting pressure of the political. There is a risk, in confronting the political, that you are taking on a weight that can fragment your images, overload your narrative.

VM: Yes, the zodiac was a little break from the political. I wanted to stand outside myself and see if I was using the political only to carve a special niche for myself. Could I work with other subjects and concerns? But, again, I felt uncomfortable and felt this was not me. The political was central to my experience, and I returned to political images when I did 'Missiles of Faith'. The pivotal image of that series was the porch with the pigeons, with the crows. And those pigeons and installations carried the same face, the same common face, the photograph of the common Kashmiri, which was meant to move and question you. It was one face, which was questioning you, the viewer.

NA: Speaking of how images question the viewer, you told us earlier about how you had to explain to the SAHMAT activists who visited your Art Heritage exhibition in 1992 that being a Kashmiri Pandit did not automatically make you a Hindutva fundamentalist. In any situation where there is a power asymmetry between the majority and a minority, it is important to safeguard the rights of the minority. If the Muslims are a minority in Gujarat and the Christians are a minority in Orissa, so too are the Hindus in Kashmir. Do you feel that SAHMAT, with all its good intentions in fighting politicised religiosity, sometimes oversimplifies the nature of religious experience in Indian society? That SAHMAT activists are not sufficiently attentive to the fact that there are forms of experience which are deeply religious but not sectarian?

VM: SAHMAT was always quick to react in safeguarding the rights of the minority, whether it was after the Babri Masjid demolition in 1992 or the violence against Muslims after Godhra in 2002, or on the persecution campaign against Husain. I found a comfort zone in participating in these activities. Because I have lived as a member of a minority in Kashmir, I sympathise with all minorities and understand their hopes, dreams, and fears. But, because India is a Hindu-majority country, I found it difficult to make a point about my personal crisis or the Kashmiri Pandit exodus, which is one of the most unfortunate tragedies after independence. It has not been addressed seriously by any political party, while it has been misinterpreted and misused sometimes by right-wing goons. My Art Heritage show was an example of art by a person from a Hindu minority in exile yet committed to secular beliefs. It is not right to say that Muslims have thrown Hindus out of Kashmir. It was a relatively few radical activists, working from a Wahhabi agenda, who were responsible. SAHMAT did not take too much time to understand this fact from my show, which was more about documenting the events in Kashmir of that time, whether it was the killing of Mirwaiz Maulana Farooque in May 1990 or the killing of

Lassa Koul in February 1990. SAHMAT may not have addressed these issues directly, but it sympathised with my position.

NA: In a recent work done for a SAHMAT exhibition to celebrate Husain's contribution, you morph Husain into a Hanuman figure. How did this marvellous stroke of cultural confluentiality come about?

VM: SAHMAT organised 'Husain at 94' at the Jamia Gallery, Delhi. I contributed a digital work, showing Husain as Hanuman flying over the cityscape of Mumbai, carrying a lighted lantern across its skies. I truly believe that he is the Hanuman of the Indian art scene!

RH: Veer, you have also done other kinds of projects, which are never discussed in the context of your career in so-called fine or high art. This is work that has the quality of public interface, is based on collaboration, and is also commissioned work. I am thinking of the floats or tableaux that you designed, for a few years, for the Jammu and Kashmir official display at the Republic Day parade in New Delhi, held on 26 January every year. What was the genesis of this project?

VM: My association with the J & K floats or tableaux for Republic Day began in a strange way. I had no previous experience of making such things. In 1997, General K. V. Krishna Rao, who was Governor of J & K at the time, insisted that the float be designed by a Kashmiri artist who was on the national stage and much more exposed to contemporary art. The resident commissioner of J & K in New Delhi called me and informed me about this, and urged me to take up the project. Initially, I was reluctant. I told him I knew nothing about the Republic Day floats, apart from having seen them on television as a kid. The resident commissioner said, 'No, you're the person for the job, I've just read about you in the newspaper'. I had just returned from Geneva, where I held an exhibition and made a presentation to the United Nations Human Rights Commission. Something about this event must have appeared in the newspapers. I told him I couldn't, and said, 'Why don't you ask G. R. Santosh, who is a very senior painter?' So Santosh and a few other Kashmiri artists were invited to make proposals. But the resident commissioner insisted I join in as well. So I drew a design titled 'Life in a *Donga*'. The *donga* is the regular river houseboat in which some of the local people actually live, the ethnic community called the Hanjis, the water people. It's not the fancy luxury houseboat for tourists. I sent off the design and forgot all about it. My design went to the Governor's committee. The next thing I knew, the committee had selected my drawing. My God! What was I going to do? So I went to meet people from the Army, since the Republic Day floats are the responsibility of the Ministry of Defence. They showed me a tractor and a trailer, which is the apparatus on which the float is mounted. That's how I became destined to be part of the same procession along Rajpath, which I had seen on TV once a year long ago. And it had to be done in a very short time. I executed the project successfully. It taught me the value of precision, collaboration, and time. The float won the first prize, which the J & K float had not won in 50 years. I didn't know this at that time. This was 1997, and the popular government of Farooq Abdullah was in power. It was a brief period of hope in Kashmir. J & K asked me to design the Republic Day float again, a couple of times, and we won the first prize again in 1999 and 2001. Such prizes, in themselves, have no meaning for me, but I was very happy to be able to do something for Kashmir.

NA: And how did you represent Jammu and Kashmir in the float? How did you go about commissioning people to participate in it? Who did you choose, and what was your curatorial approach to the float?

VM: My work on the Republic Day float gave me a great high, because militancy was at its peak at that time in Kashmir, and no one was ready to come and take part in the float, because that would mean working with the national mainstream. My policy was to bring diverse kinds of people together. Somehow, I managed, and it became a very good occasion for cultural exchange. I got folk singers from far-flung rural areas. I got the bhands from Akingam, continuing the folk theatre tradition of Muhammad Subhan Bhagat. I got Drokpa-Baltis from Kargil, Buddhists from Ladakh, Gujjars, Bakarwals, Muslims, Pandits, Sikhs, and Dogras, all together. My focus was on the composite culture of the region and the Sufi tradition of Kashmir. And you won't believe this, but appearing on Rajpath meant a lot to many of these people. Many of them did not know how to walk on a city street. Where they come from, there's no bridge over the river. And here, they saw flyovers and were amazed that there were bridges across roads. I urged the government to host more such gatherings. They help to bring people out of their cultural and political isolation. I saw the participants from Jammu and Kashmir being transformed in the time they spent in Delhi. They stayed in camps that were huge, accommodating participants from all the states. There were cultural trips for the participants, and people who had never travelled outside their district or region were now interacting with people from completely different regions. All this created an atmosphere of very positive exchange.

RH: So, the rehearsal process for the Republic Day festivity enlarged the experiential possibilities of its participants?

VM: Yes. Lots of people, some 30 to 40 people, would come every year.

NA: Because, from the outside, when we see the Republic Day parade on television, it strikes us as an official production of the image of national unity, with the art of folk performers and traditional musicians being used to cover up the deep schisms within Indian society.

VM: The preparation for the Republic Day parade gives its participants a lot of room for exchange, and I've seen people getting so emotional during it. They stay for a month in these tents which the armed forces build and form many new emotional ties, which they take with them when they leave for home again.

RH: In that sense, it is a little like a residency programme.

VM: Yes, very much like a residency programme. And my work was to design one part of it. The float could be up to 100 feet long. I would make the float 40, 60, 100 feet long, always doubling the usual scale. That was one of the changes I brought in. I had just returned from Edinburgh, Scotland, at that time, where I had had a solo show. I had visited the Edinburgh theatre festival, seen some amazing theatre there, and tableaux as well. I tried to use some of this in my designs. At the time I began to design Republic Day floats, it was done very crudely, more a play of colours rather than anything substantially thought-out. Whatever subject I chose, whether it was the donga or the Mughal Gardens, it was some heritage site or vanishing craft or cultural expression. It was like going back into the dream of my childhood. I enjoyed it.

NA: What did it mean for a Kashmiri in exile to participate in a Republic Day parade? The nation could no longer have been a site of unproblematic belonging for you. How did you envisage inserting your own crisis within the grand narrative of nationalist representation?

VM: Nancy, I was feeling miserable about not being able to visit Kashmir after I had left. So I was open to any reason to go there. This made me initiate various workshops, camps, and seminars related to Kashmir and to participate in the art initiatives of the J & K Cultural Academy. I also curated an exhibition of artists from J & K at the IGNCA [Indira Gandhi National Centre for the Arts] and at the Lal Ded Cultural Centre, New Delhi. At the peak of militancy,

I organised my first art camp in Kashmir in 1997, 10 artists with 200 security men. The idea was to share the ground reality in Kashmir with Indian artists. The second was in 2002, with no security men! Likewise, the Republic Day tableaux became a creative pretext to go back to Kashmir and explore the possibility of working together with people of different sensibility, approaching them now as a non-resident Kashmiri. I couldn't shut out hope for Kashmir, and I couldn't return to live in Kashmir; so anything in the nature of cultural advisory work gave me a sense of belonging.

NA: In fact, you have used the strategy of collaboration to publicise, analyse, and help address the Kashmir crisis, as part of your practice as an artist who is committed to the values of civil society. You have worked with human rights activists, critics, and journalists to organise symposia and conferences that provide an alternative perspective to the mainstream discourse generated by the mass media. When did you organise your first symposium or seminar?

VM: In this regard, I made a presentation on my works pertaining to Kashmir at the United Nations in Geneva, the World Social Forum in Karachi, the Wiscom conference in Srinagar, and at SAHMAT in Delhi. Also, I invited a panel of scholars to speak at a seminar during my show, 'Encounter', at the Habitat Centre, Delhi, in August 2006. I am also associated with, and actively involved in, an organisation called Yakhjah (Together) founded by Aashima Kaul. It has worked with Pandit children in exile and Muslim children in Kashmir, conducting exchange programmes and workshops in Srinagar, Delhi, and Jammu. At present, Yakhjah is actively involved with young people in Kashmir, especially those who were born and brought up under the gun culture. Circumstances have kept them ignorant about the past, about Kashmir, about what Kashmiriyat means.

RH: Your tableaux also marked the beginning of an experiment in mobile sculpture, with your Republic Day work looping back into your own practice.

NA: Was that your work for the SAHMAT exhibition, 'Art on the Move?'

VM: Yes, 'Art on the Move', organised by SAHMAT and curated by Vivan Sundaram, was perhaps the first mobile art project. It was wonderful, with young and emerging contemporaries working in different ways. Mostly, we made mobile installations that were taken on carts around the lanes and bylanes of Delhi, to schools and colleges. It was a good experience for me to explore new media for the subjects that I was concerned with. The energetic artists who participated were Bharti Kher, B. Manjunath Kamath, Arunkumar H. G., Reena Saini Kallat, Anish Ahluwalia, Sonia Khurana, Subba Ghosh, Tallur L. N., Jehangir Jani, Nicola Durvasula, and Kausik Mukhopadhyay, among others. My work was titled 'Burial' (2001). It was an invalid shikara, used to sell flowers, turned upside down, with flowers growing on it as though in a graveyard. I saw the upturned boat as a coffin, bearing the multiple self-images on both sides, with captions showing the various roles that the Kashmiri self was playing at that time: 'Militant-Secessionist-Terrorist-Fundamentalist-Refugee-Exile'. Because of this project, I began to work in multiple media and this taught me many things. It prepared me to accept the challenge of making 'The Chamber' as part of our exhibition, 'Shrapnel', which opens next month.

RH: It has been a pleasure to work with you on 'Shrapnel', Veer, and we have gone together through its various phases, as artist and curator working in concert. But I'm still curious—what was your first reaction when we proposed 'The Chamber?'

VM: Both Harsha [Bhatkal] of foundation b & g and you were keen that I should present a new project. Through our conversation, you made the curatorial suggestion that I should extend the logic of my paintings about the conflict zone into a spatial translation, into a room...

RH: A wraparound painting that you can step into and be enclosed by!

VM: After a brainstorming session, we arrived together at the final idea of the 'The Chamber'. Here I felt the presence of Ranjit Hoskote, as curator. We found a suitable site in Colaba, South Mumbai, a former office space in an old building, walked around it, getting to know its dimensions and feel, took measurements, tested the scale, and finally turned it into a chamber. I was thinking of making it into something longer. But making it a tight chamber was your idea, Ranjit. At that time, we were planning for a space that was 13 feet high. But then we shifted the exhibition venue to the Tao Art Gallery. The space was longer, but the ceiling clearance was lower. So I made the necessary adjustments in planning and executing the piece. Then we discussed another project, a series of photographs of the abandoned or re-inhabited Pandit houses of Srinagar. So I had to go back to Kashmir, though for six months, some bandh or demonstration or disturbance had prevented me from going there. It was exactly three days before the elections were to start. It was autumn. I thought I would see autumn and record the Pandit houses. I went in time for the first snowfall, and it was a treat after many, many years. I looked for Pandit houses in downtown Srinagar. This was the first time, after 20 years, that I was going to many of these places. The Pandit neighbourhoods—Ganpatiyar, Fateh Kadal, Safa Kadal, Kali Kadal, Bulbul, Lankar, Shital Nath, My Lane, Sathu Barbar Shah, Professor T. N. Madan's house, Professor Dina Nath Jogi's house, Munshi Niwas, and Lal Ded High School. Most of these houses were either locked or sold to Muslim neighbours. They speak a lot about the lost culture of the place. You have chosen 25 of these photographs for 'Shrapnel'.

RH: Because your series, 'Pandit Houses', is at once the documentation of the ruins left behind by those catastrophes, as well as a trove of images that are eloquent. They have a documentary and archival purpose, but they also have a powerful emotional quality and resonance.

VM: Yes. And there were also burnt houses, with burnt pillars still standing, just like that. And these spoke a lot too. These images also fed into my photography-based digital composite works, in which I bring together elements from these burnt logs, fragments of wood, doors, and windows. I am hoping to build these into an exhibition someday.

NA: Veer, we have also been talking, on this trip, about how being here in Jordan helps us to share in other people's crises of displacement. Nasir, our guide on this journey, is a Palestinian. His people have lived in Jordan for decades, as refugees in a half-state, not citizens yet not outsiders. As we passed one of the original Palestinian refugee settlements, you remember how the cold sun flashed on an array of tin roofs, and how the settlement was still makeshift, in stark contrast to all the modern apartment blocks we see everywhere as well as the elegant historic architecture. Your memories of the abandoned Pandit houses and your knowledge of the Pandit refugee camps in Jammu must place you in a similar strange relationship to the fluctuations of history.

VM: I tell you it's very strange, because here I am possessed by the Palestinian problem. When Nasir talks, I understand exactly what he is going through. His parents are caught up in Jerusalem, every day the Gaza strip is being bombed by Israel, and he is travelling with us across Jordan. I know exactly how that feels. His emotional state is my own emotional state. He is a professional guide, and he is giving us historical information and taking us from the Decapolis cities to the desert castles of the Umayyads to the Dead Sea and Petra, but he is not here. His mind is focused somewhere else. I can relate very well to the psyche of Palestine. But I would not have understood it so well if I had not been forced into exile myself. I understand the rootlessness of the Palestinians, the homelessness, the feeling that your jeans are getting tight around your legs and your shoes are still laced over your feet. But you have to go on sitting like that because you cannot take them off. Because you are always outside, you are never at home, you cannot make yourself comfortable anywhere. I have that same kind of feeling, I have never felt settled since 1990. In this situation, the displaced person looks around and feels: Everything has settled down for everyone, but not for me.

NA: '... This is home. And this the closest/ I'll ever be to home. When I return,/ the colours won't be so brilliant,/ the Jhelum's waters so clean,/ so ultramarine. My love/ so overexposed...' Agha Shahid Ali, in his poem 'Postcard from Kashmir'.

VM: Shahid put it wonderfully. If I do not visit Kashmir at least once a year, I feel like I am floating without anchorage. A visit to Kashmir gives me a sense of relief that lasts for six months. But that one trip is also painful, and the pain also continues.

RH: And with every passing year, you are going back to a Kashmir that is changing radically. We now have younger generations of Kashmiri Muslims growing up at home who have never known what it means to live with Hindus. Similarly, there are young Kashmiri Hindus growing up outside Kashmir who will never know what their homeland is like.

VM: Once you have pushed a particular agenda for ten years, things will not turn back. A new generation grows up, for whom that agenda and what it has created is the reality. There is no knowledge of the reality that existed before the agenda. This is tragic. Sometimes history just takes that route, and sometimes it is all thought out strategically by some people. I suggested to my

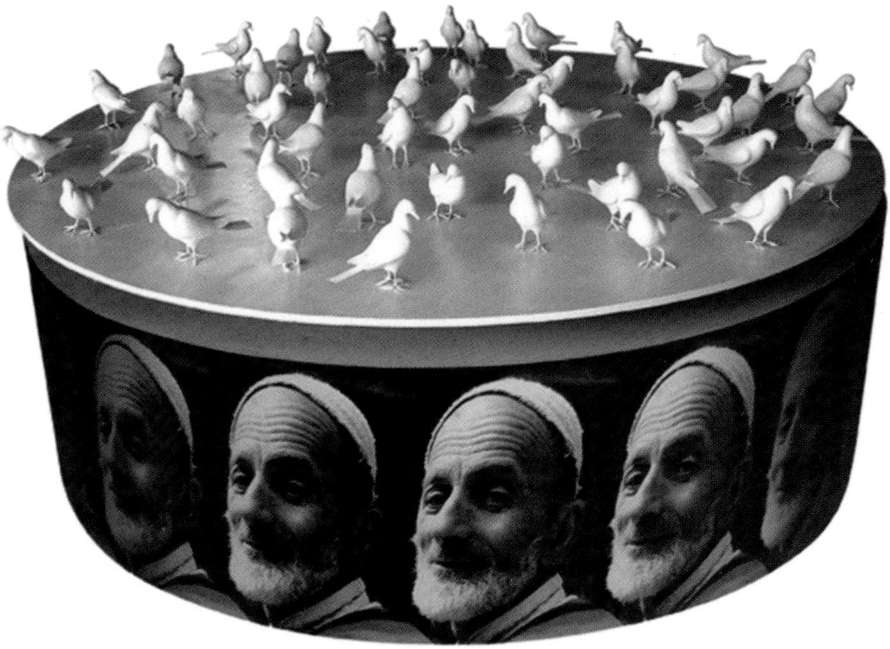

Will There Be Redemption? (2006)
Wood, photographs, papier mache

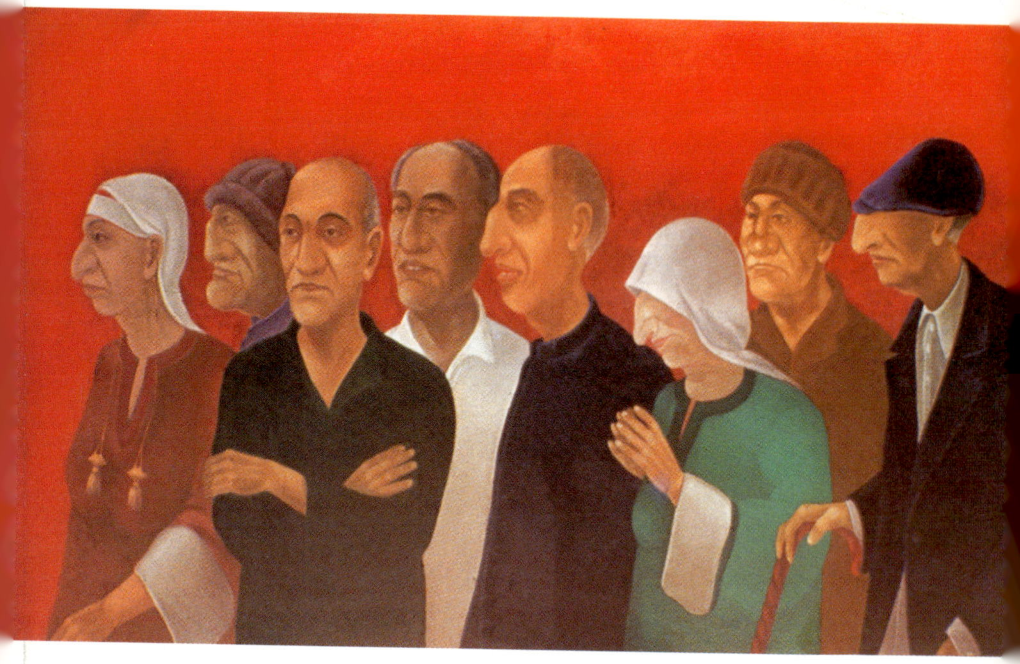

Hope Against Hope (1991)
Oil on canvas

Burial (2001)
Wood, photographs and fabricated flowers

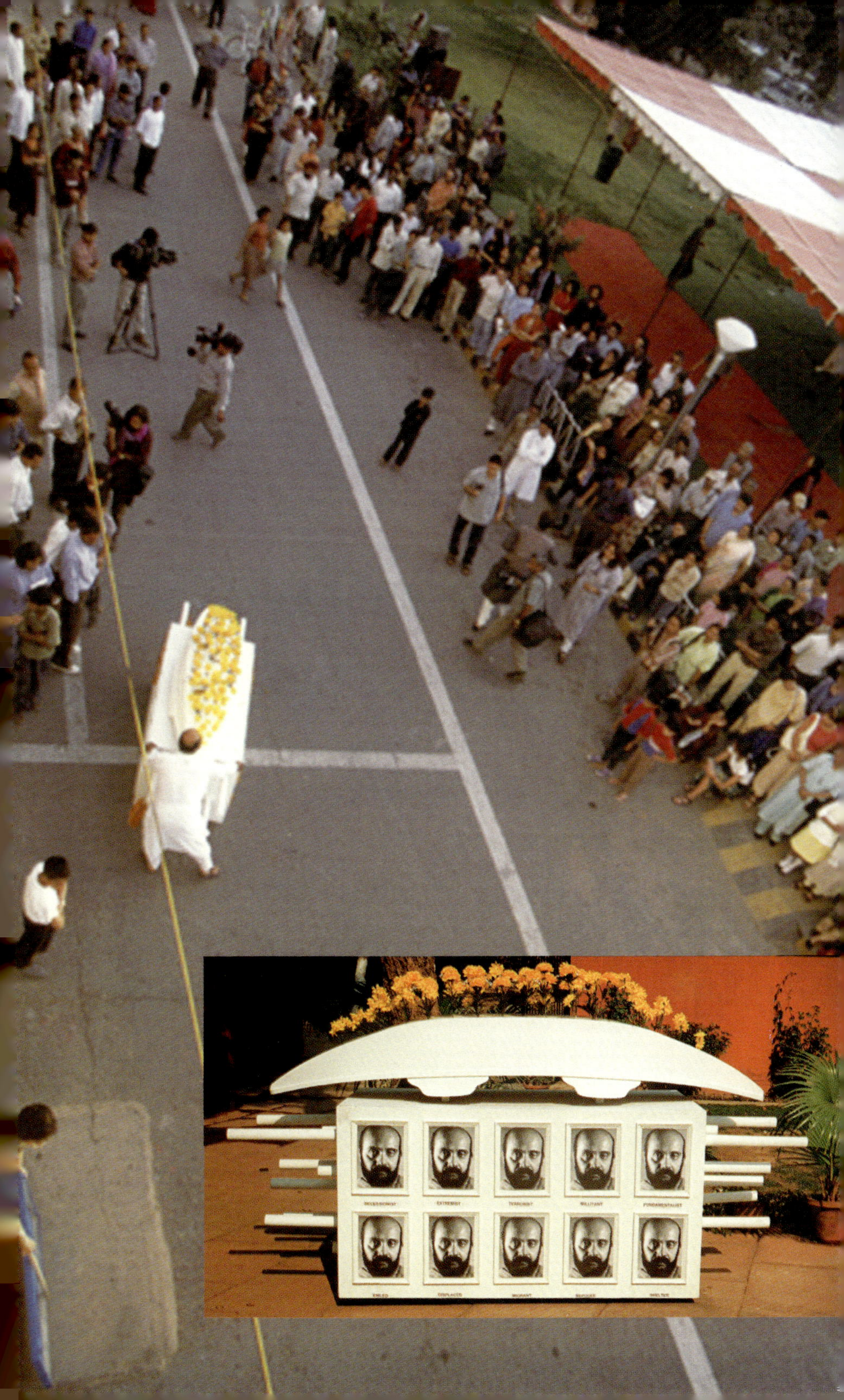
EXTREMIST
TERRORIST
MILITANT
DISPLACED

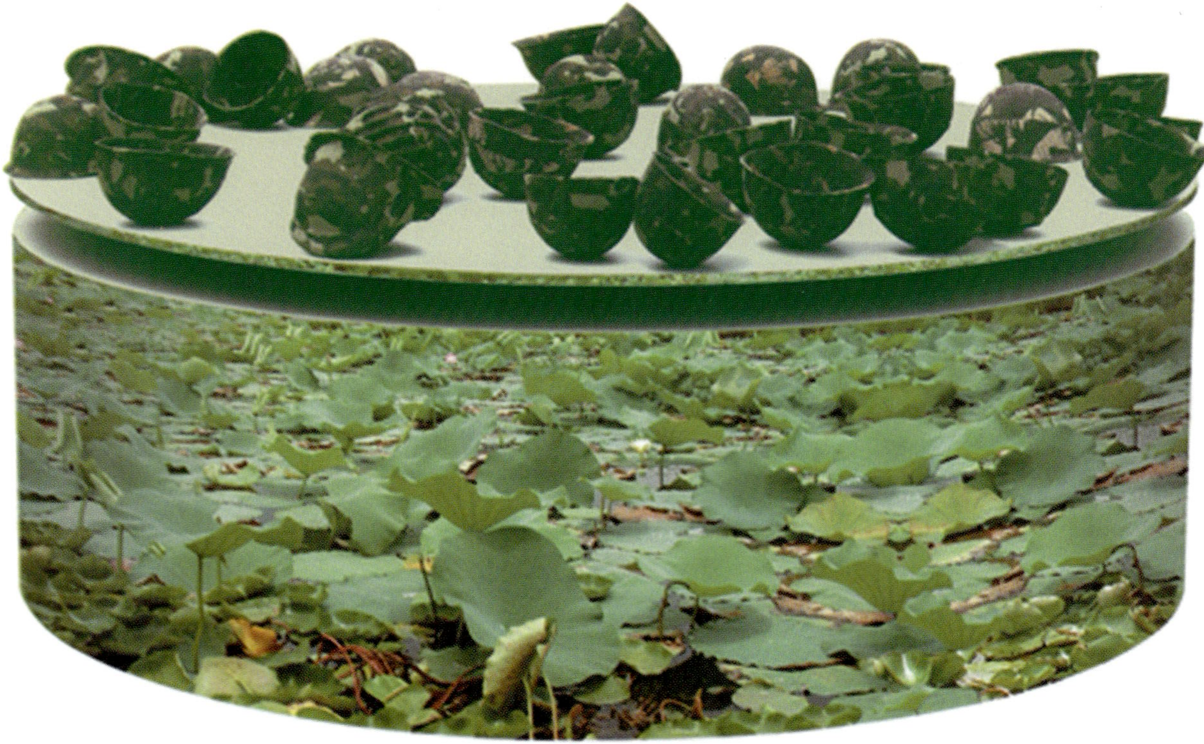

Winds of Change (2006)
Wood, metal, digital prints

niece that she should visit Kashmir. She did. But on her return, she asked me why one needs to go there. Instead, she prefers to go to Goa. She was born outside Kashmir and has no sense of connection with it. Imagine, this is the change in the sense of belonging after just one generation. The feeling of Kashmir being the homeland will never come back. The same is true for young Kashmiri Muslims who live in the Valley. They have no sense of connection with the old Kashmir. It is up to our generation to do something about it. I have many Muslim friends in the Valley, and we still have common beliefs, points of reference, and shared forms of communication. I feel very different when I go to Kashmir now. So many things have changed without anyone really noticing them—forms of greeting and salutation, idioms of speech, public holidays. People don't understand how such changes creep up on them until they become part of normality. Whether these are subtle changes that happen in daily behaviour, or forceful changes made by people acting in accordance with larger plans, larger timetables of change.

RH: Both Kashmiri Islam and Kashmiri Hinduism are also being changed forever by these disturbances, the diaspora of the Pandits and the rise of Wahhabi ideology in the Valley. Both Kashmiri Islam and Kashmiri Hinduism were so special, and soon, they will be part of that vanished Kashmir which we will only read about in books and see in old documentaries.

VM: Definitely. Even Kashmiri Hindus are changing and adopting all kind of practices from mainstream India. Also, there are no Kashmiri priests in Kashmiri temples any more. They are run by priests from north India employed by the armed forces. They do their own *pujas*, and don't follow the special rituals of Kashmiri Hinduism. We have Bhairav and Kali *pujas*, with special offerings. All this has disappeared from Kashmiri temples.

NA: And how has the community regrouped in exile, coped with displacement, and attempted to preserve its own cultural trajectory?

VM: There have been periodic world Pandit conferences and other meetings of Pandit associations. Some groups have turned towards a right-wing Hindutva stance, and I have kept myself away from such forces. In 1992, after the exodus, a Kashmiri Pandit social organisation wanted to raise funds for an international conference to draw attention to the plight of the refugee camps in Jammu. So I made an image of Sharika, a Shaivite goddess popular with Kashmiri Pandits, for them. There was an existing calendar image of Sharika, but in a Hema Malini posture, made in Sivakasi, in South India. I tried to localise Sharika in terms of her features, attire, and background. I showed her with Hari Parbat, the sacred hill in Srinagar, in the background. One of my friends took the image to the Dalai Lama, who blessed it. My Sharika image was released at Siri Fort auditorium. Many people from outside India attended. The atmosphere was charged and everyone was crying. An old woman from Germany began to tell me how she too had become a refugee when Germany was defeated and broken up at the end of World War II. Somehow, my Sharika image has won magical acceptance, and many Pandit households have it. The reproduction is still being sold by the social organisation, to help the refugees with health care and education.

RH: Veer, it has been a privilege to be taken deep into your emotional and artistic life.

NA: Thank you, so much.

2

Haji Ali

Mumbai (28/03/2009)

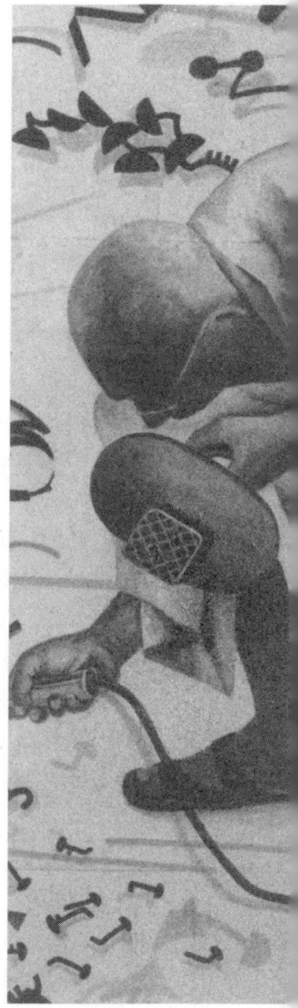

Haji Ali
Mumbai

Ranjit Hoskote: Veer, you must be relieved and happy, now that we have opened your solo exhibition, 'Shrapnel', and are sitting here in an apartment looking out over Mumbai's Worli Bay, looking out at the island-mosque of Haji Ali with the tongue of land over which pilgrims cross to it from the shore. It is four in the afternoon, but perhaps it would be correct to greet you with a cheery 'Good morning!'

Nancy Adajania: Veer, I have just seen a programme on CNBC this afternoon, which featured your exhibition, 'Shrapnel', as well as a small capsule on the Sri Lankan Tamil singer who lives in London and goes by the name of MIA. The themes of both 'Shrapnel' as well as MIA's music have to do with the human costs of war. While MIA was talking about displacement in the context of the civil war in Sri Lanka, you were talking about the wages of a violent politics as suffered by the Kashmiri Pandit community. What I thought the programme lacked, however, was an understanding that artists do not simply have generic or universalising responses to specific political crises. An artist also has his or her own political stance. This is extremely important in MIA's case, because she is actually a sympathiser of the LTTE's cause. This was never mentioned on the CNBC programme. Although the anchor repeated the word 'politics' five or six times on the show, among generalities about war and violence, you were never told what MIA's political position really is. In the same vein of inquiry, Veer, I would like to ask you what your politics is, vis-à-vis this exhibition?

Veer Munshi: This happens all the time on television. The focus is on getting a few quotes from the speaker, so the framework is not given the correct importance. Mine is a politics of keeping memory alive, not as nostalgia but as a sign that history is different from how it is being presented today by different kinds of interested parties. History is not what ideology tells you. It has its own voice. The artist must listen to that voice, translate what it is saying, and communicate that to others. 'Shrapnel' is founded on my relationship to Kashmir and its disturbed history of the last few decades. It has come into being because, whenever I go back to Kashmir, I feel as if I am going to the ghost landscapes left behind after the end of World War II. These abandoned houses, walls overgrown with grass, broken windows, sometimes with activities going on around but not inside them, provoke the imagination. Such silent houses speak out loud. This journey began two years ago, when we three met at the reception desk of the Broadway Hotel in Srinagar. I was there for a conference organised by the NGO Wiscom; you both were there to attend Khoj Kasheer. And Ranjit suggested that my reference photographs of house could be works in themselves!

RH: Yes. We wanted to take a boat ride down the Jhelum with you the next day, but our schedule became too crowded, unfortunately.

VM: You both wanted to see the vista of Srinagar from the river. No one has ever asked me about a Jhelum boat ride before! Most tourists who visit Kashmir, they know nothing about the inner world of Kashmir. All they see is the picture postcards; they want to go to the Dal Lake, Gulmarg, Pahalgam, and Mughal Gardens. Even today, for viewers, this is Kashmir. That day, when you said you wanted to visit the mediaeval inner city of Srinagar and see the city from the Jhelum, I was enthusiastic to accompany you, since you have such a great sense of history.

NA: To bring these thoughts back to 'Shrapnel', were you afraid that your exhibition could be hijacked, at the level of reception and interpretation, by right-wing political groups? And how did you formulate a strategy that prevented your work from being susceptible to such acts of co-option?

VM: There are danger areas. It has happened many times with my works, before. But it was very different this time. Here I am working on the abandoned houses of Kashmiri Pandits and referring to their fate directly. Normally, I would have balanced this by dealing with other affected communities. But this time, it was not a question of balanced representation. The language of art-making that I chose, the possibility of photography that Ranjit pointed to, helped me to evolve beyond that question. The politics of place is important as content. But, for 'Pandit Houses', testing the strength of my new language becomes equally important. Earlier, I was working with the possibilities of symbolism and allegory in painting. And sometimes, in the past, when I have tried to balance many things, I have lost my balance and lost the fibre of the work. With the act of photographing what is already powerfully there, with no extra commentary, I have moved to a new position. Art is not only about expressing your problems, it is also about working on a significant language.

RH: Veer, there is something compelling and powerful about the ruin. This is a subject that has fascinated artists for a long time, and has been meditated on by historians and critics under the signs of the Sublime and the Picturesque. Artists in a long lineage across the centuries, including Caspar David Friedrich, Arnold Böcklin, Anselm Kiefer, and Huma Bhabha, have reflected on the ruin. In the last few days, for some reason, I have been thinking a lot about Guru Dutt's 1962 film *Sahib, Bibi Aur Ghulam* where a discovery that is made in the ruins of a great mansion, by someone who had played a role in that house in its days of glory, is the lynchpin of the story. The boy who grew up in that house comes back as an architect and discovers the skeleton of a woman who had been murdered there.

NA: He identifies the woman from the bangles on the wrists of her skeleton, and this clue triggers off the entire narrative of memory, decline, loss, and a melancholy redemption achieved only after that lifeworld has vanished into thin air…

RH: Absolutely! In the same way, I find your evocations of Pandit houses working as clues, prompts that start off a narrative. At the surface level, as we have said, these photographs have an archival and documentary feel. But they also encode a haunting sense of anguish, which is all the more powerful because often the only signs of life are the puppy that is running in the street or the king-hawk that has settled on a perch somewhere near the top of the house.

VM: When I visit Kashmir now, the first fact I must confront is that it is my home but I have no home there. I have to stay in a hotel. It is such a pathetic experience. The first time I went back to Kashmir after leaving, and had to stay in a hotel, I checked in, quickly checked out. Then went to another and checked in, checked out. I checked in and out of ten hotels until it was dawn. When you move back into a place that has changed so much, you try and go back, layer after layer, over the memory of how you lived in these houses. I can imagine each part of these houses, their interiors, and each detail. In one of them, we had wonderful feasts, in another, we played as children. I did not enter any of these houses when I was photographing them, sometimes because somebody was living there, and I did not want them to get suspicious about what I was doing there. You have to take these photographs with a lot of care. I realise there are no human beings around, in my frames, and it is true. It was normal to me there. Here in Mumbai, many people have questioned me about why there are no human beings in 'Pandit Houses'. They are not there because they are not there.

NA: In your series 'Pandit Houses', there are smaller as well as large epic-scale photographs. The smaller images work like preliminary sketches for this exhibition. They are a little distant, slightly cold, and present frontal shots of the buildings. But as we move into your epic frames, we see the real drama of the ruins and the unpeopled landscape. In the image of the Lal Ded High School, you also have a small proletarian houseboat, a *donga*, on the river—this points up the contrast in scale between the large shell of an emptied-out architecture and the small but resilient river-craft, the afterlife of the school abandoned during the exodus and the continuing desperate resistance that the water people put up at the margins of survival. And the shards of glass in the school's windows rhyme with the green and blue hues of the Jhelum's water. Would you like to talk about how you decided on the framing of these landscapes?

VM: Most of the photographs were taken directly, without too much preparation, in the environment. Sometimes, I had to take the pictures in a hurry, because I didn't want to attract too much attention, and sometimes I was able to take more time, to work with a tripod and make a proper frame. The seasons, because Kashmir has four proper seasons, created the biggest challenge. When I shot in summer, it didn't work at all—in summer, the sky is a beautiful blue, there are cotton clouds coming in, and Kashmir looks its picture-postcard best. I tried in spring, and again the beauty was too obvious. Finally, it was in autumn and winter that I found magic. In autumn, the clouds are sporadic, the sun gets filtered through these layers, the light is fine and soft, there are no strong shadows. In winter, the snow casts its own light. You don't need to use filters. The bricks in many of the houses look beautiful in such conditions, with their honey colour. These are very old bricks, used for building forts and shrines.

RH: Using a very old Kashmiri technique, with mortar, brick, and stone?

VM: Yes, an old Kashmiri technique. Even the stones are held together with mortar. The house itself was built to allow for a feeling of communion. It had these balconies. In the porch, you could sit as a family and have a treat or a feast together. Or sit together for a tea ceremony, Kashmir's answer to the Chinese and Japanese! Kashmir's bakeries were so famous, one kind of bakery for the morning, another for the evening. Whether it is a Pandit or a Muslim, the culture was the same. We didn't always have a Pandit *mohalla*, sometimes it would be one Pandit house among ten Muslim houses. But the culture was shared and composite. These houses will not be rebuilt and history will be buried. The whole civilisation that played a great role in the history of Kashmir will be forgotten. In the frame you talk about, Nancy, it suited me to have that little boat. That particular school, the Lal Ded High School, is not a typically Kashmiri piece of architecture. It is built on the lines of British colonial architecture. The boat is a sign of the locality, the spirit of the place. And I show just half of the boat, so you are right, it becomes a sign of how life is struggling to speak itself in Kashmir.

NA: In the other photograph that you have of the Lal Ded High School, you have chosen to shoot from a low angle, almost as if you were shooting the photograph from the level of the Jhelum. It is deep winter, and the whole structure looks as though it has been propped up by a mountain of snow.

VM: I'm happy you like that frame! For that photograph, I crossed the Jhelum in a shikara and found a position from where I could get that angle and perspective. It gives a wonderful view, with the snow-melt and those steps projecting out.

NA: You have also shot your own neighbourhood, your old lanes. Does somebody else live in your house now?

VM: I shot some of the bylanes, but my own house has been burned down, disposed of, and a new structure has been built over it. So there was no point taking a photograph of it. But I shot some of the houses on the way to where my house used to stand. There is Dr. Gassi's house. And Professor Madan's house, which is a remarkable house, with grandeur and charisma, a real heritage structure that has so much to offer from the historical or architectural point of view.

RH: Some years ago, Salim Baig of Intach had commissioned a group of architecture students to produce a very comprehensive heritage listing for Srinagar. But I don't think there is any legislation to protect heritage buildings there yet. This is truly tragic, because Srinagar is one of the most beautiful mediaeval cities of South Asia.

VM: But no one knows this, I tell you. No regular tourist who comes to Srinagar knows it is a mediaeval city. That is why I was very touched that day when both of you talked about this. I thought, God, no one else comes to see this side of my city!

RH: On my previous visit to Srinagar, I spent some time on the other side of river from Shah-i-Hamdan, and looked at some temples commissioned by Diwan Bal Kak Dhar in the early 20th century. These temples were closed, walled in with bricks. You have to scramble over the walls to get inside. So, within Srinagar, there is a secret city waiting to live again, waiting to invite guests!

NA: Were there parts of Srinagar that you did not visit, even before the disturbances began?

VM: Yes. Some of these areas in Srinagar that you mention, I have never visited them. We used to call those neighbourhoods lacunae or war zones. This time, too, I was sceptical and worried whether I could go there. Then my friend Muzaffar Ali from Srinagar took me to all these places, and told me which house belongs to whom, and its history, and what had happened there. He is aware of the history and geography of the place, and of all the mishaps that happened around these houses, shrines, and heritage sites during the turmoil.

NA: Because the architecture is so beautiful, the subject could have lent itself easily to a simple juxtaposition between grandeur and ruin. But you have been able to steer away from this binary, and bring a certain human scale to the buildings. Even though we see nobody, we never forget the drama of the people who once lived here. I think this human scale is at work in your photographs, even when you take low-angle shots to create a sense of awe. You approach these structures with a sense of prayerfulness, infusing them with a measure of dignity and grace. Your photographs don't look like coffee-table images, but like the work of somebody whispering a *dua*.

VM: Definitely, yes. When I lived there, I did not notice these aspects. Now, as an outsider, I see the solace, grandeur, desolation, and what you call the remembered drama of the lives that were led there. Images are born in strange ways. There is a triangle—you as the artist, your subject, and your language. Sometimes, you have to lose your subject to find your language. And sometimes, you have to lose your language to find your subject.

NA: We have often seen women, sometimes also men, crying and talking to themselves in *ziyarats* throughout the Valley, trapped in a loss that can never be redressed. And I have wondered how we could find images through which to convey such an abyss of loss. When I look at your very quiet images, which do not have a stated location and are not provided with labels identifying the neighbourhood or the former owners, the quietude of these houses is a twin of the lonely cries of the people in the *ziyarats*.

VM: Yes, you have put it wonderfully. The women are crying, the houses are silent, but what is lost will never come back. The people and the houses are both becoming withered and weathered by time. Slowly, we will document these things, which are not easy to talk about.

NA: Kashmiriyat is perceived as a construct today, produced by intellectuals and writers who cherished the composite culture of Kashmir. How do you look at Kashmiriyat? Was it a belief, an attitude, a form of being that was embedded in everyday life when you were growing up? Do you believe that Kashmiriyat has been destroyed or can it be reclaimed?

VM: When I was growing up, there was an idea of Kashmiriyat but also a fear about what our relationship with it was, as a minority. Who was giving a shape to Kashmiriyat? Once I had finished school and begun to have a better understanding, I realised that there was an invisible fear. Our parents would tell us that maybe we would have to leave Kashmir one day. The culture and language were almost the same for Pandits and Muslims, but there were systematic political shifts attempting to pull them apart. There was a class problem as well. The Pandits were educated and of the elite and were mostly teachers and professionals. Many Pandits were landowners, and the opposition to the landowning class could also have been asserted in religious terms sometimes. The campaign of 'land to the tillers' was applied vigorously in Kashmir. Did it happen in other parts of the country?

RH: Actually, it did, in a very few districts, especially in Orissa and coastal Karnataka. In 1952, we lost our lands in North and South Canara. Because, as Saraswat Brahmins who had migrated south-westward from Kashmir, we too were a migrant elite minority and among the first landowners to be vulnerable after Independence. It is the same story as in Kashmir. Elsewhere in the country, *zamindari* continued in other forms, surviving the politically motivated rather than reform-based demand for land to be given to the tiller in the early 1950s.

VM: That is how it happens. To be a minority is a strange and difficult thing. I would like to retain Kashmiriyat in the broad sense of a composite culture. But the idea of Kashmiriyat is losing ground to the Wahhabi ideology and Islamising strategy of the separatists. In a few decades, centuries, Kashmir will be totally different. When people move out, they never return. History says so. Your people, the Saraswats, left five and six hundred years ago, and have not returned. Two hundred years ago, the Nehrus and the Rainas and others left. They never went back. I have left 20 years ago, and it doesn't look like I am going back. I would love to, but unfortunately, there is never a reverse migration. I would love to live in a Kashmir that reflects the philosophy of Lal Ded and Nund Rishi.

NA: When you live in Mumbai or Kolkata or Chennai, Kashmir seems very distant. Mumbai wakes up every now and again to global terror when there is a bomb blast or the horrific invasion from the sea that took place on 26 November last year. But the daily reality of terror attacks, curfews, blasts, and army patrols seems to belong on another planet. How do you plan to bridge the distance between your artistic concerns and your audience in metropolitan India, especially Mumbai?

VM: This time, with the 'Chamber', I wanted the audience to become participants in my work. I wanted to bring them right into the work, not just look at it from the outside. The 'Chamber' is not confined to Kashmir. I have used images from Afghanistan and Palestine in constructing it. I have this image of an Afghan boy emerging from a blast. Unlike television, which creates a momentary impact, I have tried to create images that will continue to provoke, and not fade away.

RH: Both 'Pandit Houses' and the 'Chamber' are effective in themselves yet are also open-ended. They are both projects that will take new avatars as they go along and find different contexts to inhabit. 'Pandit Houses' is both a suite of images and an ongoing archive installation. The 'Chamber' is made of paintings but is an environment, partaking of the quality of theatre. In some way, these projects are metaphorically Kashmir Brahmins—who have, for hundreds of years, migrated whether under pressure or for other reasons and extended themselves into other forms. Veer, I find your projects very organic to the way in which Kashmiri Brahmins have conducted themselves throughout history. This wasn't planned, but it is amazing that it has happened this way!

NA: In fact, the Saraswats have an idiomatic usage that refers to the ever-present threat of exile in everyday life.

RH: Yes. It is a turn of phrase that I have not heard in any other language. If your house happens to be in disarray, with piles of books lying everywhere, or if you haven't dusted the carpet for a long time and the curtains are just being taken down to be changed, a visiting relative might say, 'My God! It looks like the house of someone who is about to flee'. It shows the extent to which the experience of being a refugee is hard-wired into the language. It pops up in turns of phrase and different ways. The idea of diaspora is very strongly there. It is present in the imagination and the language.

VM: Yes, it passes from generation to generation and becomes part of the vocabulary.

RH: And meanwhile, the language at home is under threat. Some days ago, I was telling both of you about the very enlightening conversation I once had with the great Kashmiri poet Rahman Rahi, who said that, despite all the talk about Kashmiri independence, not one of the separatist outfits had ever done anything for the Kashmiri language, literature, or culture. I found this quite unusual, because most sub-national or nationalist movements emphasise these aspects of culture, whether it is Ireland or the Indian freedom struggle. Once again you will find that the separatists in Kashmir have contributed to damaging the Kashmiri culture. In the worst days of the terror, militants were known to mutilate and kill bhands.

They imposed censorship on poets, singers, and dancers. They banned music, dance, and cinema. And the Kashmiri language is being edged out in favour of the kind of Urdu that is heard to the west of Kashmir. So, you know exactly where that agenda is being imposed from.

VM: The militants were against cinema, and cinema houses were burnt down. The girls' school was burnt down. It was not only the Pandits they targeted. They wanted to damage the basic fibre of Kashmir.

NA: And there have been attempts to push women behind the veil.

VM: That is what Wahhabism does. It tries to damage the Sufi belief system of the Valley. Although Kashmiris in general have not accepted the burqa, nor have they stopped women's education, a great proportion of Kashmiri Muslims want progress. But what the people want, and what the politicians hope for, are two different things. What is the nature of the freedom that Kashmiris believe they will get? That is a very big question.

RH: And let us not forget the more than one lakh Kashmiri Muslims who have also gone into exile. You see them everywhere. You see them on the beaches of Goa and Kerala selling handicrafts. The militancy also destroyed the economy of Kashmir.

VM: The economy is destroyed. Most of the affluent Muslims send their children away, to study and make new lives elsewhere. Politicians of all shades make promises that they cannot keep. What is the role of an artist in such a situation?

NA: You have asked yourself that question many times on your journey. You have mustered up the courage to talk about issues that others have either avoided or on which they have fixed views. You have used different degrees of proximity and distance to approach your subject and your audience. And while politicians in crisis situations always ask you to become a *shaheed*, martyr, the artist wants to be the *shaahid*, the witness.

VM: Yes, the artist wants to be the witness rather than the martyr.

NA: Which would you prefer to be?

VM: The witness! '*Shahaadat*' is a good word, martyrdom, but...

RH: ... everything depends on who is using it, and for what cause.

NA: Who is asking for martyrdom in Kashmir? You have to know whose tune you are really playing to, when you think you are sacrificing yourself to a universal revolution.

RH: And usually those who ask others to embrace martyrdom are careful to remain safe and happy at home while other people die. In Srinagar, when you visit the Mazhar-e-Shauda, the Graveyard of the Martyrs, you will see hundreds and hundreds of young Kashmiri Muslims who were asked to give up their lives by leaders who are absolutely safe and comfortable, still publishing manifestos, issuing calls, setting agendas. While the boys from Bandipore, Budgam, Shopian, Baramulla, and Wandhama will never go home again.

VM: What would you call these leaders? Witnesses?

RH: I would call them manipulators.

VM: I will call them opportunists.

RH: We will take up this discussion again, at another point. Veer, Nancy, thank you very much! It was a very disturbing and moving conversation.

VM: Thank you.

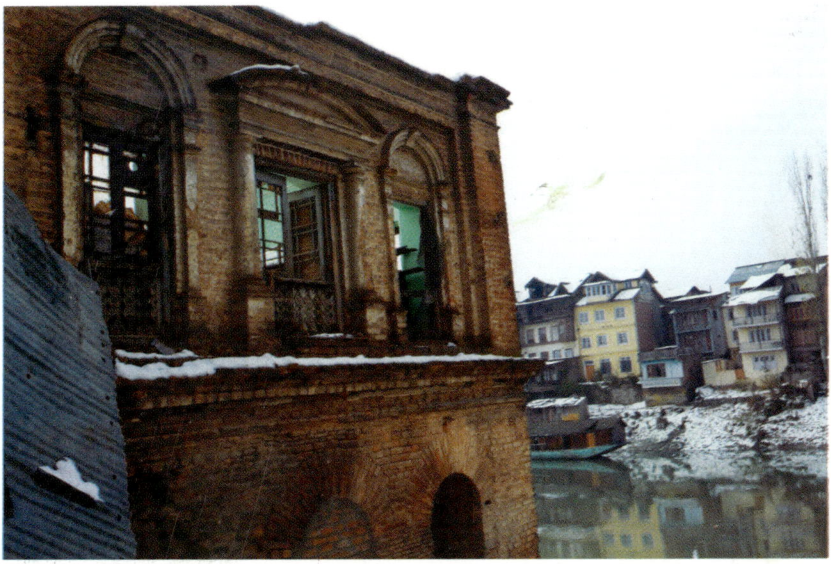

From Pandit Houses (2008)
Photograph on archival paper

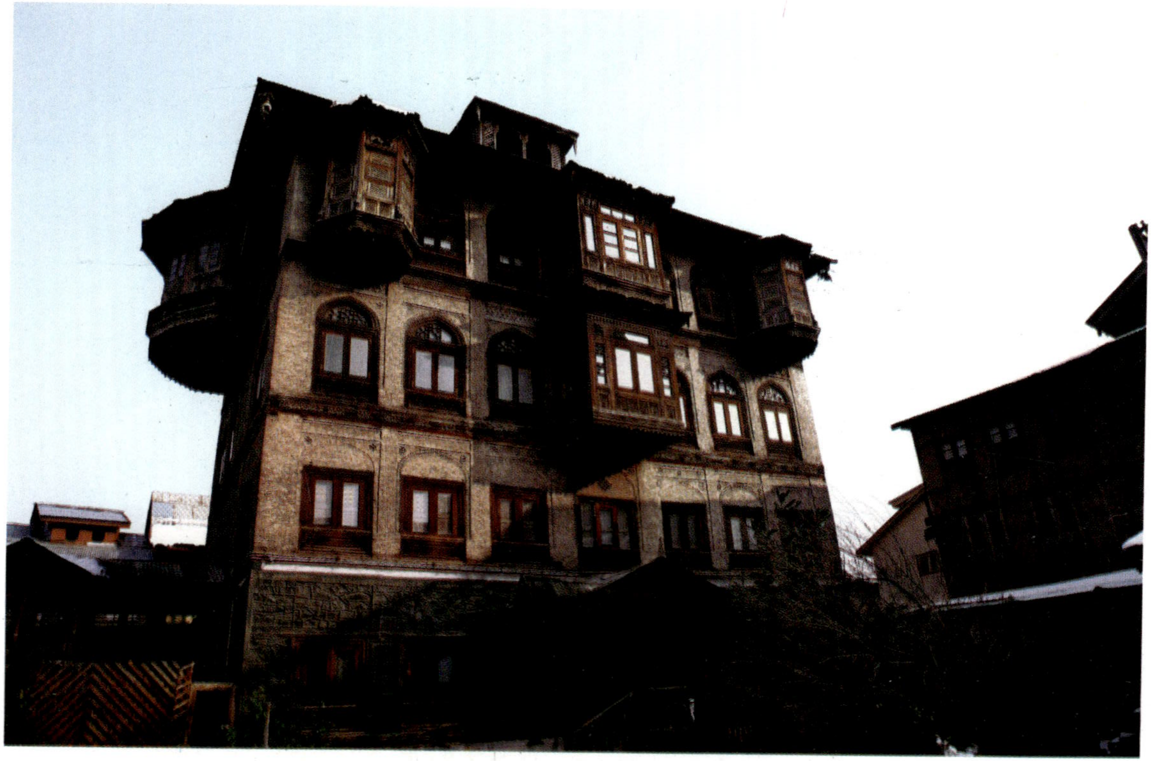

From Pandit Houses (2008)
Photograph on archival paper

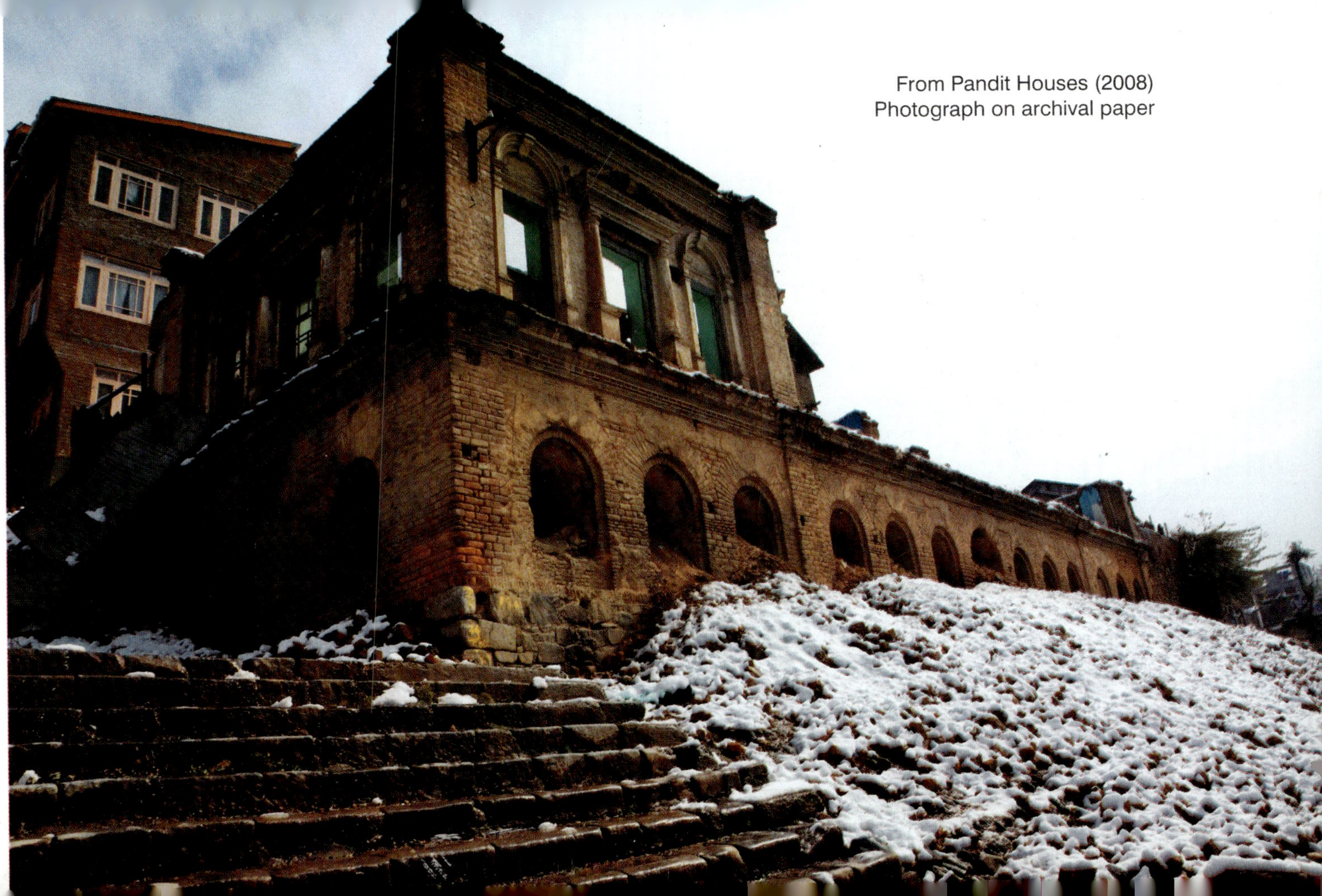

From Pandit Houses (2008)
Photograph on archival paper

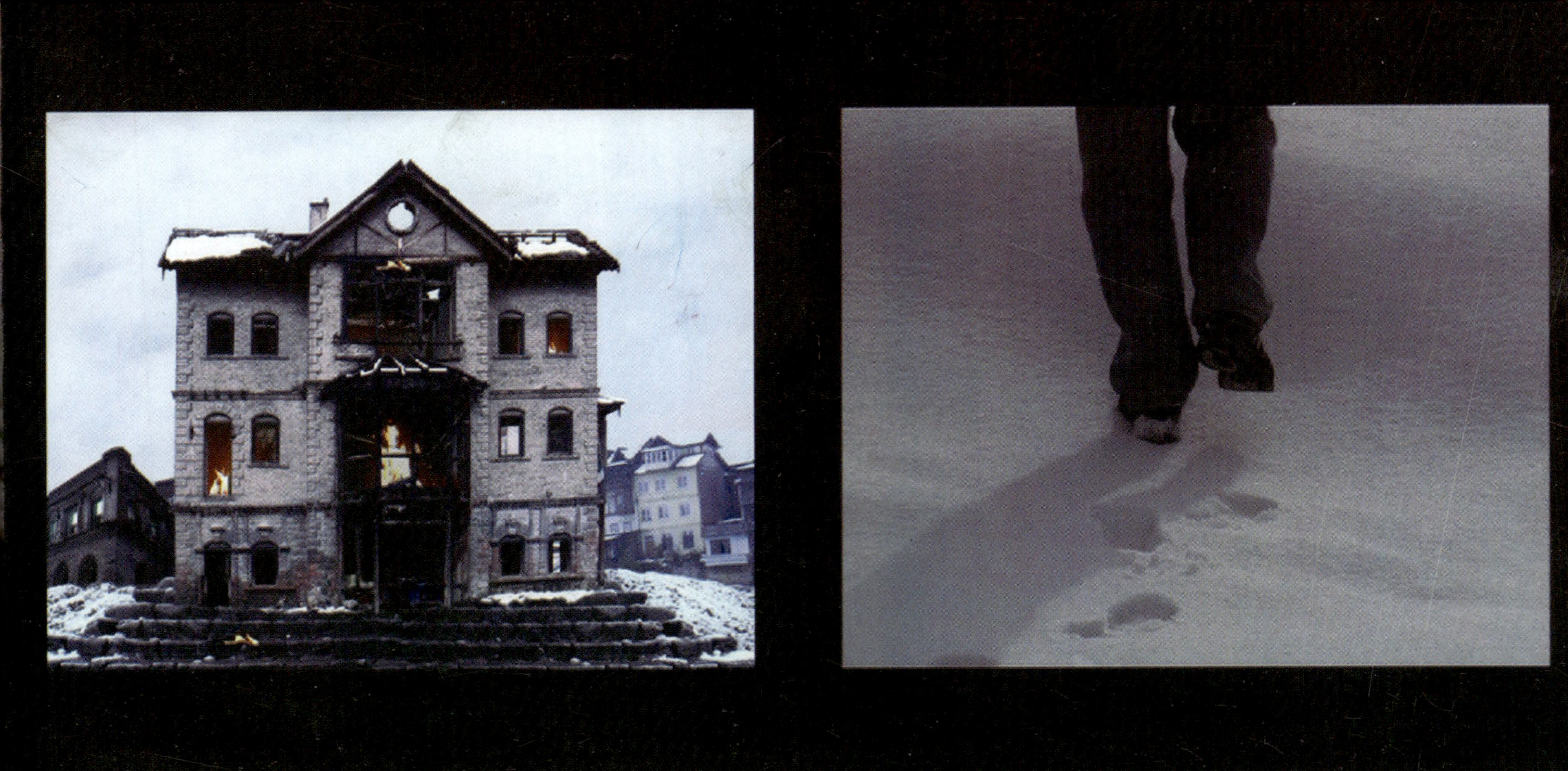

Leaves Like Hands of Flame (2010)
Still image from 2-channel video

3

Haji Ali

Mumbai (25/09/2009)

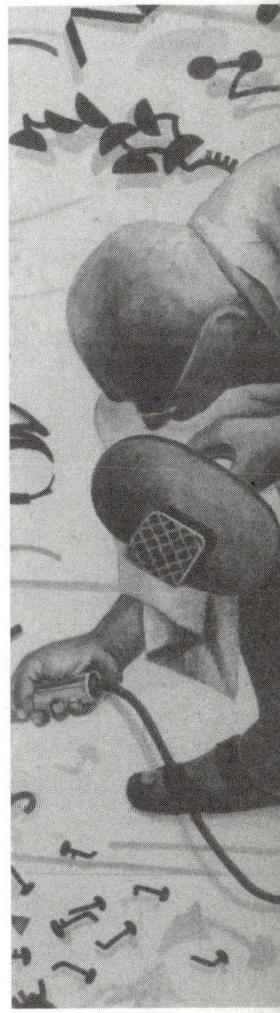

Haji Ali
Mumbai

Ranjit Hoskote: Veer, our previous conversations have been contoured across the terrain of the political. We have discussed the intimate relationship between political crisis and the emergence of resonant works of art. This evening, Nancy and I would like to explore the excitement of your student years in Baroda. What were the artistic and intellectual discussions that reverberated through Baroda when you were studying there?

Veer Munshi: I was fortunate to be a student in Baroda during the late 1970s and early 1980s, which was a very important period for the Faculty of Fine Arts at the M. S. U. I remember the arrival of the 'Trimurti', as we called them—the trinity of Gulammohammed Sheikh, Vivan Sundaram, and Geeta Kapur—two artists and a critic who became very influential and gathered together a group of colleagues across India, the artists and thinkers who became known as the narrative movement. They created a stimulating atmosphere. We see the results in the work of several generations of contemporary artists who studied in Baroda during this period. The narrative movement was very inspiring, even if it later narrowed down the possibilities of art-making a little. We all took it up because it gave significance to the images that we were drawing. It gave us access to the aspect of content, rather than only competence of form and perfection of style.

Nancy Adajania: The narrative turn in art, elaborated in Baroda during the 1970s and 1980s, was intended to sensitise Indian artists to ideological choices and questions of representation, the ethic of responding to the regional and immediate, and the politics of representation as applied to working-class figures. Were you and your generation electrified by these ideas?

VM: I found a new order of being, in which I could pursue my painterly interests and at the same time, I could research my social, cultural, and political surroundings. Also, we painted many things that were directly linked with the choices of our teachers and their colleagues associated with the narrative movement. For instance, Sudhir Patwardhan was painting trains at that time, and I also drew and painted trains, because I enjoyed the freedom to create such images.

RH: Those are wonderful paintings. In 'Train', which Sudhir painted in 1980, he inserted an intriguing Francis Bacon-style head into the everyday lives of commuters on the Mumbai local. And in 'Accident on May Day', painted in 1981, he recorded his apprenticeship in chromatics and figuration to the Mexican muralists, and his gradual disillusionment with the politics of the orthodox Communist Left.

VM: Yes, those paintings. Earlier, we would only have painted as a formal practice, but the artists of the narrative movement, Sudhir Patwardhan, Bhupen Khakhar, and Gulam Sheikh, made us think about the image and its relationship to what it was representing, and how it was representing a certain kind of local life and culture. Since, culturally, I was in Gujarat and surrounded by Gujaratis, the subjects were all around us. I found I could peep into their culture. During 1980–1981, I painted Pensioners' Park in Kamati Baug, with the roadside men's toilet bearing the sign, '*Purusho maate*', 'For Men'. I drew and painted *maamis*, professional mourners who wore black saris with red borders and went everywhere as a group. They were fascinating to look at. Driven by curiosity, I would follow them to a house where a death had taken place, and where they created a morbid atmosphere by beating their breasts and crying in strange voices. That's how I realised what a professional mourner is and does, someone hired by the business community to add to the tragic dimension of death as social loss.

NA: So the *maami*s were like the *rudaali*s of Rajasthan in Mahasweta Devi's story, translated into a film by Kalpana Lajmi in 1993, women who expressed, as ritual theatre, the grief that upper-caste women mourners could not show in public. Your act of painting the *maami*s was an act of investigating the layers of a society and its culture of public behaviour, self-representation, approval, and legitimation. Would you say that the narrative movement disclosed some anthropological possibilities to young artists, even if that term was not used at the time?

VM: I think I learned the word *rudaali* from the film, more than a decade after I painted the *maamis*. I felt a strong connect with Kalpana Lajmi's film.

NA: So your figure now had a social context, which it resisted in some ways, yet from which it also took definition.

VM: I would say my work was narrative, and yet not part of the narrative school. I had a strong interest in the life, customs, and traits of people.

NA: Which of your teachers, would you say, contributed most to your own journey as a young man and an artist?

VM: K. G. Subramanyan was of more theoretical bent and emphasised the structure of art works, how art practice connected both with historical experience and physiological experience, how paintings and sculptures were built up from different elements. His teaching took us to the heart of art practice, and his lectures were very powerful. I remember many of his lectures as events. He would come without formally preparing any subject, but would start with a topic that interested him, and give you the benefit of a deep and elaborate study. On one occasion, he started with the subject of vision, and talked about the chemistry of the eye, the science of optics, retinal experience, how we perceive what we perceive, and then connected all this with colour, perspective, vision, and illusion in the visual arts. That kind of education had a huge impact on us. Every teacher has his own way. We got a lot from KG at the knowledge level, but we did not adopt his artistic language.

RH: KG was and is that rare figure, a practising artist who makes wonderful art and is also a theorist with a powerful grasp of cultural history, who embraces plural positions and contradictions and doesn't reduce history to a cosmic justification of his personal artistic choices.

VM: But KG left for Santiniketan quite soon. After that, Vivan came to teach us. With his teaching, our understanding of art practice grew more conceptually oriented. Theory and ideology were discussed more deeply. There was a lot of discussion about social issues and cultural patterns, and the artist's relationship to society, rather than only questions of how to achieve finesse in handling paint and canvas. What was the history and present of the figure we were drawing? Vivan would sit with us and discuss the higher questions. He and Gulam were on the same wavelength, and the themes of their lectures were linked. Shaikh taught perfectly, speaking and demonstrating to the point as regards practice. But he also gave us enormous inputs about the Rajput miniature tradition, the Mughal tradition, about Italian painting. In those days, Baroda was buzzing with activity and its environment attracted students from all over. There were students from Kashmir, Kerala, Assam, even Bangladesh, Malaysia, and England. You learned so much about other people's states, regions, countries. By learning about each other's cultures, we grew in understanding. Our art education was not only about practising a skill. It was also about expanding our human horizons. Friendly relations between students and teachers were valued, as was freedom of expression. The studios were open day and night. Many students from that period have gone on to become significant presences in contemporary art—Dhruva Mistry, Ravinder Reddy, Surendran Nair, Nataraj Sharma, Valsan Kolleri, Rekha Rodwittiya, Anita Dube, Jayashree Chakravarty. N. Pushpamala, V. Ramesh, and many others. Jyoti bhai, Jyoti Bhatt, was another great teacher who taught us about art but also about life, and continues to do so. As students, we found him very skilled in his technique on canvas and in print-making, and a fine photographer. I recall Jyotsna ben's, Jyotsna Bhatt's pottery class, Dhumal's helpful nature in the graphics studio, and Ram Chatpar's patient clay modelling. Chatpar's inputs on sculpture were quite noteworthy. I recall Dr. Ratan Parimoo's archival references in his long lectures on art history, and Vishnu Kumar Bhatt's obsession with Ananda Coomaraswamy—Bhatt taught us Indian Art and Culture as a subject in the 2nd year of our BFA course.

NA: Didn't Nasreen teach you as well? Her minimalist style and monastic demeanour must have stood in contrast with your other mentor figures. More than a teacher, she must have been an auratic presence.

VM: Nasreen's presence was very important for us. She received us as first-year students when we entered the Faculty of Fine Arts, and gave us our foundation. She was very sensitive, and made us simplify ourselves. We learnt a lot from her about how to live in close touch with the environment. She made us sweep the floors of the studio and the grounds, which irritated some of us at the time. Only later did we understand that this was not a cleanliness fetish but a spiritual discipline. We understood the true meaning of her studio practice only much later, after we had passed out.

Her teaching was precise, never sterile talk. She would never put us to sleep during her lectures. She would walk in, pick something up, and observe it minutely as if under a magnifying glass. Then she would ask us to make drawings of objects. So, while sketching and painting, we also would work with minute attention, and certain features of the object would come into view, which we had not observed earlier, although they were not invisible. If anything appeals to you, she would say, draw it, keep drawing it until you have every detail of it in your mind. Before Nasreen opened our eyes, we would think academically about rendering a shape, but not going into the detail of what we saw, or why we saw it that way, and so we produced sterile drawings. Nasreen showed us how to pick up the image like a seed, to sow it, and grow it with our senses and in our minds, to go deeply and attentively into everything we did.

Nasreen taught me perspective drawing. She made me sit in front of the Maharaja Sayajirao Museum for months; it was a huge building with many vanishing points. I would work on my drawings, and she would come only rarely to review my progress. But when she came, she would ask what responses I had had to the building, the site, the relationship between architecture and its surroundings and people. That was Nasreen's way of teaching and it was wonderful. I began to love drawing. She was very special, and always built up a personal rapport with her students. She was not just a teacher, but a friend who guided us in unobtrusive ways. Once, we got into an argument and the next day, I did not attend her class. She came to the hostel. I was so surprised that Nasreen was at my door. Her style was so subtle. She did not say anything to me but just implied that this was not done.

NA: And how did you respond to Nasreen's art?

VM: I used to enjoy her way of drawing, but I never related to it. Her work is abstract and perfect. But for me, images, with all their flaws and associations with the experienced world of sensations, became important. But she gave me a love of drawing for its own sake. At the moment, I am very fond of the work of the South African artist

William Kentridge. I saw his work at the 51st Venice Biennale in 2005. I was fascinated by the scale of his work, and his methods. He combines drawing, video and animation. He merges political images with a deeply imagined inner reality.

RH: Yes, Kentridge's installation shown at the 2005 Venice Biennale was very special, with its double title, 'Day for Night' and 'Journey to the Moon', presented as a homage to the high-spirited, visionary cinema pioneer, and science-fiction artist Georges Méliès (1861–1938). These were nine short 16-mm and 35-mm films, looped on DVD and shown like an exhibition of moving paintings. There were two wall-size projections, and the other films were presented as two diptychs and a triptych. Kentridge has also extended himself into tapestries, and he has been developing theatre and opera pieces as integral manifestations of his art practice for a long time. His animation-oriented video points towards a new kind of cinema, really.

VM: When I work on a drawing, especially when I am drawing with a brush as I often do now, I feel my art speaks better. That is how I painted the 'Chamber' for 'Shrapnel', as a continuous fluid drawing of landscape and debris punctuated by human, animal and bird portraits, rendered across the four inside walls of a rectangular space.

NA: Veer, you graduated from Baroda in 1981, the same year in which the landmark exhibition 'Place for People' was mounted. It was organised by a collective comprising Geeta Kapur as critic and the artists Vivan Sundaram, Sudhir Patwardhan, Bhupen Khakhar, Nalini Malini, Gulammohmammed Sheikh, and Jogen Chowdhury. Did you visit this exhibition, either in Mumbai or in New Delhi, its two venues?

VM: No. I didn't go to the exhibition, but we knew about it, of course. The participants used to come to Baroda, everyone used to come to Baroda, so these ideas were very much in the air. It was so stimulating, something new was happening or being planned all the time.

NA: Baroda was clearly an environment of learning that took in far more than classroom teaching. As at all great institutions, the informal discussions and long evenings of debate in the hostel would have been as important as the lectures, if not more so. And there were also the periodic art fairs which were staged like popular *melas*. K. G. Subramanyan was the lead figure encouraging students to work with craftspersons.

VM: Definitely. The art fair was a huge event, and it was the most enjoyable and most educational part of our Baroda experience. We loved, especially, KG's toys, children's books, and many other things that he made or inspired others to make. We would assist the teachers to organise the art fair. Huge workshops were temporarily set up, and the art fair would be a major creative event. I haven't seen anything quite like our Baroda art fair anywhere else. The teachers gave us a lot of encouragement. Some of us would do theatre, somebody would make shadow puppets, some would make wooden toys, and some would come out with graphic work like calendars, posters, and books. But everything that was made had both a creative element and was usable.

NA: Through the art fair, you were shown the possible relationship between fantasy and functionality. These did not have to be opposites. The hierarchy between high art and low art, fine art and craft, gallery culture and public culture was broken.

VM: Yes, exactly. Within the context of the art fair, we could use different materials and media, and all would be accepted as legitimate modes of artistic expression. We became familiar with many other media than painting, and many formats and scales of work. We learned how to work together, to combine resources, and organise events. KG led the way in showing how art was not confined to a single accepted medium like oil painting or bronze sculpture. It was not that you had to start with painting and end up with painting. With that training, we are today much more open to a range of media. Now, for example, I am working with digital media and with video. You can make perfect art using any material or combination of material.

NA: You must have interacted with many different kinds of people at these art fairs, people from outside the field of art, people who were not from the university circuit?

VM: It was fun, as well as an extension of our practice as artists! We were interacting with thousands and thousands of people. Art may not have had a large market in those days, but the things we made for the art fairs sold like hot cakes. People liked these art fairs very much, so they were organised every two years. Also, another regular occasion for wide interaction was the Navratri *garba*, which was very important to us, the collective dance with its festive beat. It was a cosmopolitan occasion, with people from different backgrounds, cultures, languages, and ideologies coming together in a cross-cultural celebration.

NA: As a student in Baroda, did you ever feel like exploring other kinds of content or other media?

VM: I enjoyed pottery as well as working with clay, but not beyond a point. So I took to painting. We used to make a few environmental works in those days. We had the opportunity to work with different, fascinating materials, but these were put aside. The syllabus kept coming back to canvas. The figurative concepts were the main syllabus. In those days, we did not use the word 'installation', but installations were made. The form acquired a different strategic value and art-historical position in the Indian art world much later.

When we were students, we simply enjoyed trying out things that were different from what the syllabus had structured for us.

RH: At that point, from the academic point of view, was there not an awareness of developments in global art practice and art history from 1965 onwards? Did your teachers make you aware of the strategies of the conceptualists, or installation strategies, or all the shifts of consciousness associated with what came to be called the postmodern condition? Was there any discussion in Baroda, at the formal academic level, of what Arthur C. Danto has usefully termed the 'post-historical condition' that emerged after 1965 and the plurality of choices and modes of art, as well as the anxieties of location and direction for artists, that it made possible?

VM: Since there was no Internet in the 1970s and 1980s, information on anything, much less on development in global art practices, was hard to come by! People travelled far less than they do now, and even international art exhibitions in India were few and far between. Although we did have frequent visits by well-known Indian artists, who showed slides of their work and interacted with students, I don't really think there were structured discussions or purposeful efforts to disseminate awareness of the 'shifts of consciousness' produced by the postmodern condition. Painting, sculpture, and graphics were pretty much straitjacketed in their respective compartments, but that was probably the situation in more or less all the major art schools. Some of the Western artists whose work did have an influence on students' work were Hockney, Kitaj, Max Beckmann, John Davis, and Howard Hodgkin, to name a few.

RH: Quite right, but during the time that you studied there, were the major shifts in 20th-century art between 1945 and 1965, and through the 1970s, brought across by your teachers?

VM: Of course we were certainly aware of the major shifts in 20th-century art. The art history classes were taken seriously, to help and equip the students not only with theoretical inputs but also a sense of historicity. But all this knowledge didn't quite translate into students adopting different strategies in their own work. All that came much later. The teaching was very different, as I have said. It did not revolve around a still life kept on a table with drapery and a bottle with flowers, like it was at many other art schools. Baroda broke that model. And although it was the home of the narrative movement, with its emphasis on a new figuration, Baroda was not just a trend-house. The narrative movement may have been the big movement, but as far as Nasreen was concerned, as far as KG was concerned, there were other journeys to be taken.

NA: Ranjit, in a way KG's democratisation of art practice, both in terms of pedagogy and praxis, served as a prompt to opening up the Indian art scene to the possibilities of the 'post-historical condition', where no single medium or lineage or style was privileged over the other. But the attitudinal freedom that KG offered artists, liberating them from the narrowness of medium-specificity, was not supported by a large, enabling awareness of debates in international art regarding practices such as performance art, happenings, installation art, and conceptualism. A huge gap existed between the artistic desire to transcend the hierarchies of medium and lineage, and the knowledge required to translate that breakthrough into productive expression. This gap was bridged in India only from the late 1980s onwards, as a new generation of artists and critics saw themselves as participants both in a regional and a global art scene. Even though artists like Vivan had studied in the UK and travelled in Europe during the late 1960s, participated in the 1968 students' movement, and been exposed to performance art, installation, and video art, they all seemed to have fixated on painting on their return. Veer, I find this strangely perplexing. How do you respond to this?

VM: Vivan was trying to transmit new thoughts and open up new areas for us, which was wonderful and encouraging. But I think that was not the priority of the narrative movement at that time. I think they were trying to revive elements from the tradition, as Gulam was doing with the miniatures. As an artist, it was Bhupen who we found to be the most forceful. Although he seemed to be very easy, casual-looking, he was dead serious about his work.

RH: Could the emphasis on narrative painting as the preferred mode of artistic revolution have alienated some students, who may have had investments in abstraction, minimalism or other pictorial choices?

VM: Narrative became a trend, or rather, an effort was put into making it a trend. If you didn't fit in with it, you weren't there, you didn't exist. I did not see myself fitting into a readymade ideology, and wanted to discover an art-making language for myself. As a student, you are emotionally sensitive, not yet sure of your direction in life. You have to mature in order to outgrow the sense of being ignored, and make your own thrust. But many artists felt ignored. Some of them left Baroda and the art world forever, others remained and joined in a political conflict between different ways of seeing and being. By attaching yourself early in life to one ideology or artistic programme, you confine yourself to one segment of experience and miss the chance to explore many other things. This is the negative effect of trends and movements. I am not amazed by the availability of new media, but I am suspicious of anything being made into a trend without proper thought. Whoever joins the trend becomes fashionable. Then it slows down or gets washed out by the next trend, and where are you left? You have to have the strength to ignore the watchdogs of trends and follow your own spirit.

RH: Veer, Nancy, thank you for a most enriching conversation.

4

Popular Prakashan

Mumbai (26/09/2009)

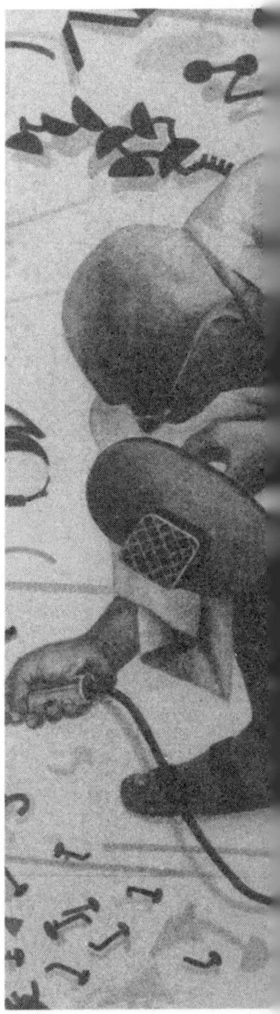

Popular Prakashan
Mumbai

Nancy Adajania: Veer, we are sitting here in the offices of Popular Prakashan, surrounded by books and manuscripts. A publisher's office is part library, part archive, part studio floor for the production of new ideas. Last evening, we spoke in detail about your student years in Baroda. In this conversation, we would like to take you further back into the archive of the self. What was the kind of work that you were exposed to in Kashmir, before you shifted to Baroda? What were the visual stimuli for art students and young artists there?

Veer Munshi: We had a strong watercolour landscape tradition in Kashmir. We would take a boat and go out to a conventional spot on the Jhelum, or go up to the mountains. Sometimes, we would spend a whole day looking for a view-point, and then paint a watercolour of the vista. That was the style in Kashmir. We had many well-known watercolourists like D. N. Wali, Mohan Raina, Nisar Aziz, and S. N. Bhat.

Ranjit Hoskote: Kashmir certainly lent itself to the cult of the picturesque during the 1950s and 1960s. With its snow-capped mountains, crystalline lakes, vibrant local culture and special status within a newly independent India, it was so much the Other to the Gangetic Plains and the tropical peninsula. There was great scope for the exotic when you were dealing with Kashmir, and also for chromatic play and the unabashed pursuit of natural beauty.

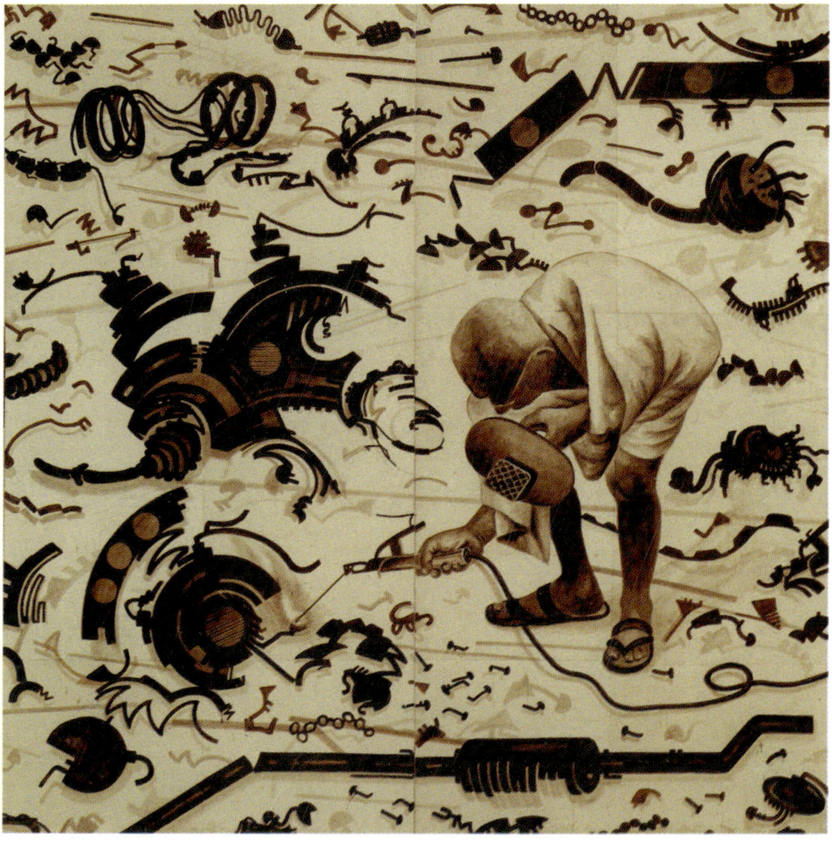

The Patient Welder (2010)
Acrylic on handmade paper, pasted on board

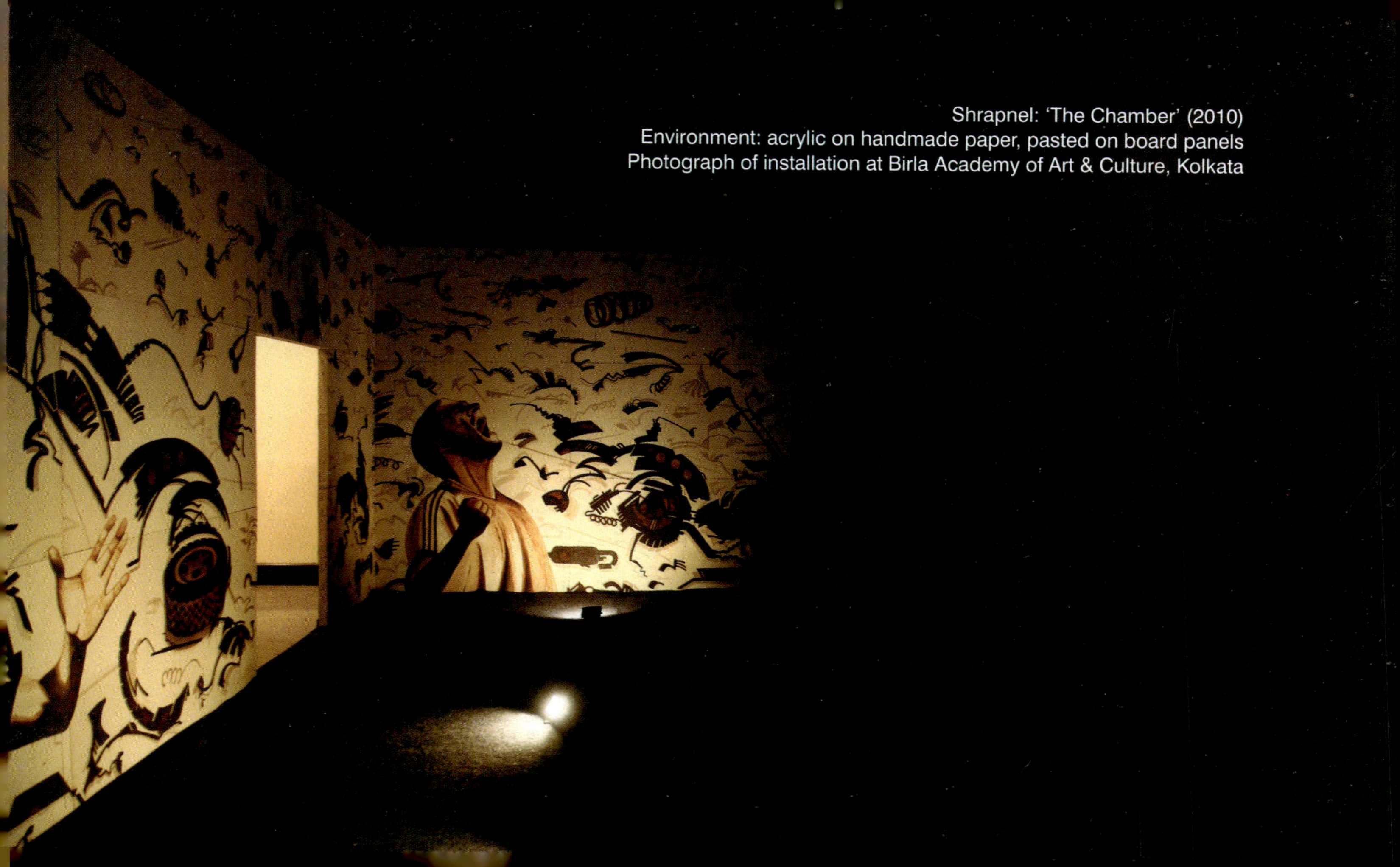

Shrapnel: 'The Chamber' (2010)
Environment: acrylic on handmade paper, pasted on board panels
Photograph of installation at Birla Academy of Art & Culture, Kolkata

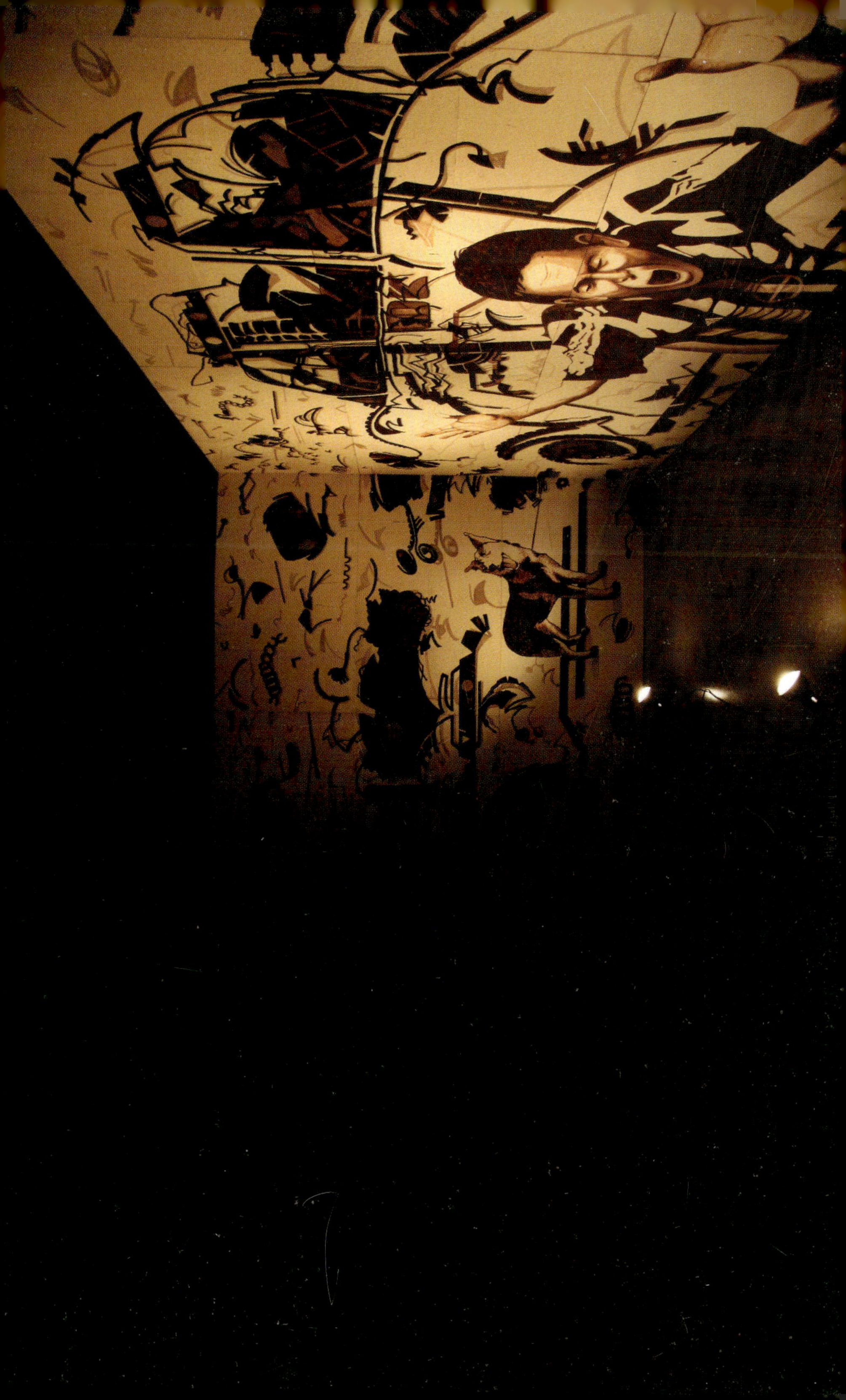

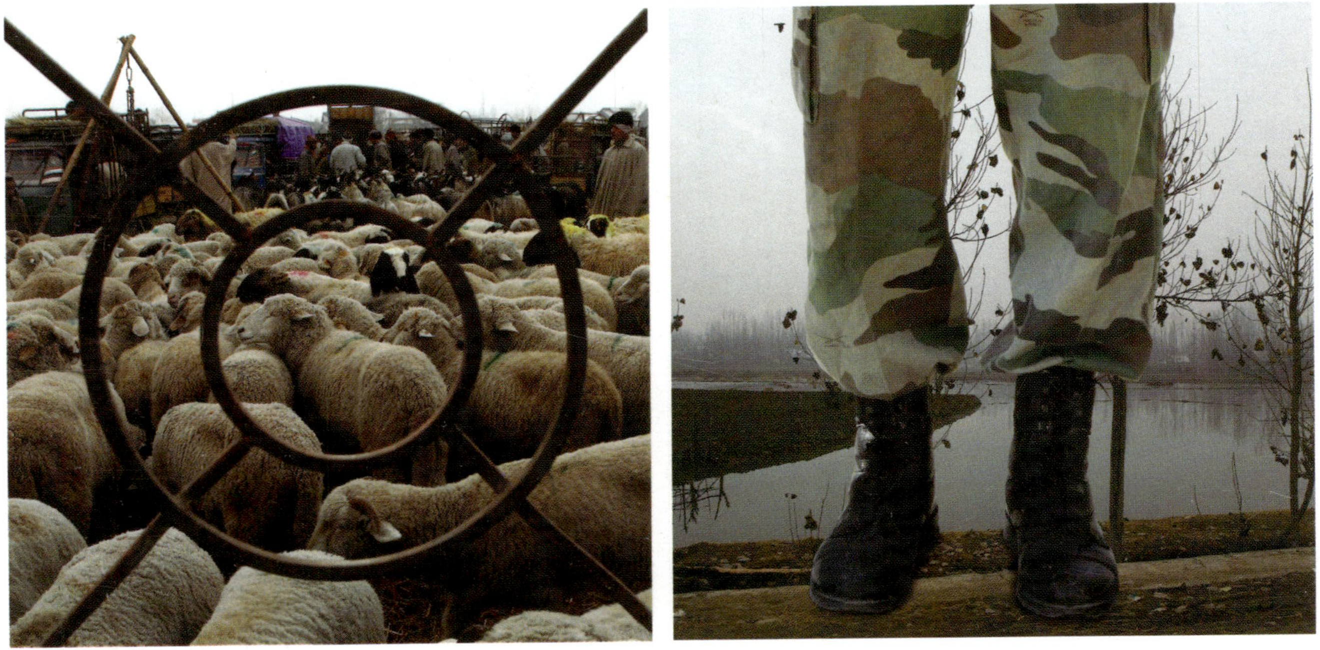

Who Committed the First Sin? (2010)
Photograph on archival paper

Raza's 'Kashmir Landscapes' represent the best outcomes of his early period, before he switched to the *bindu* and the *mandala*.

VM: Raza came to Kashmir often in the 1960s, as well as Husain and Bal Chhabda. They came for the month-long camp that G. R. Santosh began to organise every summer for the J & K Cultural Academy in Kashmir. Almost every significant Indian artist participated in these camps. They would come, stay and work in Kashmir for a month. Without the daily pressures of life in their own cities, they would make large numbers of paintings, quite a collection. In those days, economic conditions were not what they are today. No one took flights. All the artists came by train. As students, we used to go to these camps. It was great fun to watch Husain, Ram Kumar, Bal Chhabda, Bendre, Sankho Chaudhuri, Manu Parekh, Manjit Bawa, Gulam Sheikh, Paramjit Singh, among others, painting and sculpting. We would accompany them to the market, be there for the interactions between the artists and the public. It was a passion for us. We grew up in this period of cultural renaissance, and the art camps were a great inspiration for our generation to pursue art.

NA: Were the annual art camps, convened by Santosh, part of a larger cultural scene in Kashmir? Or were they an exception?

VM: The art camps were very much part of Kashmir's lively artistic and intellectual culture during the 1960s and 1970s. I tell you, it was a period of cultural renaissance. Art, music, poetry, and radio were very active, and there was a strong theatre movement. There were good pubs, where discussions took place among artists, writers, poets, intellectuals, theatre people, and musicians. This activity was concentrated around the mediaeval inner city of Srinagar, which is situated on the bank of the Jhelum between Badiyar-bala and Fateh Kadal. There were many theatres, known as *rang-shaalas*, in this stretch, which were popular venues to perform contemporary folk music and drama. The long period of unrest in Kashmir and the advent of Wahhabi forces have wiped out this renaissance, even its memory. The present generation of young Kashmiri artists and art students has no access to this past. As a result, their work suffers a lack of historical dimension and confidence. You must have seen their work.

RH: Many young Kashmiri artists are quite isolated and, naturally, greatly preoccupied with the urgencies of their political situation. They do not enjoy the necessary repose and nourishment which artistic activity needs in order to flourish. You can achieve a great deal under pressure, but not under overwhelming pressure. They face many problems of infrastructure, exposure, and interaction with colleagues outside Kashmir, which must be overcome.

NA: But Ranjit, Veer, you must also remember that younger artists in Kashmir are making their presence felt on networks in virtual space, through new socialities that bring together like-minded individuals across the globe, via Facebook, YouTube, websites, and blogs. We have seen the work of many young Kashmiri photographers that way, as well as the graphic novel-based work of Sajad Malik. Due to the situation of conflict, they are indeed isolated on the one hand. But on the other hand, they are able to tap into networks beyond the domain of conventional art-making, such as the SARAI readers' list, where people based in Srinagar, Helsinki, Sydney, Amsterdam, Gaza, and Mumbai can all share insights and opinions.

VM: I agree that networking in virtual space plays a great role in these circumstances, yet an exposure to contemporary art practice has its own importance. By and large, many young artists in Kashmir are not exposed to the major developments in contemporary art.

NA: During Khoj Kasheer, the first Khoj workshop residency held in Srinagar in 2007, we met some talented Kashmiri artists who lacked a proper context for the making and reception of art. Veer, you have often spoken of taking exhibitions of contemporary art to Kashmir, to expose young artists there to current debates in art and art history. But considering the volatile political situation there today, do you think the conventional exhibition proposal is less of an option?

VM: We just have to expose art students in Kashmir to different media. There is a lot of potential there. I hope the shutdowns that we see in Kashmir today are temporary. We must think of the long term.

RH: Would that long-term vision also include the possibility of your own return, however temporarily, to work in Kashmir? You have been experimenting, recently, with video works based on an experience of crossing the Jhelum.

VM: Yes. I've been going again and again to the Jhelum when I'm in Srinagar. I have been shooting both sides of the river. I am trying to see the Jhelum from Satisar and see how it flowed in the old days. How did the Valley get its shape, and is there any reality to the myth of the sage Kashyapa, and how the Valley of Kashmir was originally a deep lake? Is the city a structure that is floating on the river? Does it remain alive only because people give it life? These are the strange questions I am asking myself.

RH: Do you see your practice moving gradually from painting towards video and installation?

VM: I am getting into these media more, and enjoying them. I am working on two or three works together, at the moment. And we have been discussing the video work juxtaposing my journey home with the image of the abandoned house. That will be the extension of the 'Shrapnel' concept into video.

NA: You indicated, some time ago, that you would like to use animation in this video. How has that played out?

VM: Yes, I have been working on the animation element of the video. In this video, I am on a road that goes back into Kashmir, and some of the psychological events will be rendered in the form of animation episodes. There may be a fire bursting out from a roof. From time to time, a window frame or a piece of twisted machinery may fall. I am not sure of the exact details, but this is the general idea.

NA: Recalling your 'Chamber' from the last exhibition, I found it very interesting that you use many machines of destruction, which suddenly turn talkative and yet also become absurd in their multiplicity of moving parts and junk elements. They seem to have emerged from fairytale lore, and they also remind us of the infernal machines, the war machines designed by Leonardo da Vinci in his role as a military engineer working for the potentates of Renaissance Italy, the condottieres, and the papal princes. Many years ago, when we were travelling through the Loire Valley in France, Ranjit and I went to see the villa in Amboise where Leonardo had spent his final years. There, we saw and were enchanted by the models of his war machines and flying machines.

VM: I have also been fascinated by Leonardo's war machines! The first time I picked up lots of books of Leonardo and went to see an exhibition of his works in Italy, I became caught up with his drawings of machines. At that time, I did not relate it to my own work, but when I began to draw images of vehicles blown up in a bomb blast, and armoured vehicles and artillery, this experience of viewing Leonardo's drawings came back. Then I started to learn about his flying machines. It was not the technical side of his work, but the drawing part of it that I found so fascinating. It hadn't occurred to me earlier that you can make something visually powerful out of machines, even broken-down machines. Machines can look crude, yet they are aesthetically so beautiful. Gradually, I started visiting a scrap market, a huge scrap market where they even had Patton tanks and helicopters.

RH: Where is this house of wonders?

VM: This is in Rajouri Garden in Mayapuri, in Delhi. I have kept the photographs of various kinds of scrap that I have found there. I found different kinds of patterns in the scrap, chose images from there which I could incorporate into a series of mixed-media works. There are broken cars, pieces of heavy machinery, metal from domestic utensils, all kinds of burnt and broken things, which I am very attracted to!

NA: It must be like walking on a battlefield, amidst the debris of war!

VM: Debris—you said it, exactly! All broken things speak to me, they have something to talk about, some story to tell. A house is not a house unless it has been burned down; a motor car is not a motor car unless it has been blasted by a bomb. The sad truth is that we discover the true value of things after we lose them.

NA: The scrap objects in your work also suggest caricatures of the human form, some lost echo of anthropometry. When I walked around your 'Chamber', I thought I was dealing with human beings who had been trapped in some other form by a brain on edge. Your images of debris take on an enchanting yet also a sinister quality.

VM: The debris speaks to different people in different ways! What happens is that, when you take an exact photograph, you think you have got the object. But it doesn't work that way. I have to take thousands of photographs before I find a form in the debris that is alive. I don't draw and I don't make any reference sketch. I just allow the object to seep into my head, so that I can start painting it from one end to another. My debris pieces are mostly monochromatic—one surface, one colour, one brush. I take the brush and I start. I feel I can cover thousands of meters like this! Because it is like writing and I am writing a script. There is no plan to it. I may use an element of a figure, as punctuation, but mostly I listen to the demands of the pattern and the surface.

NA: Like spontaneous writing?

VM: Yes, like spontaneous writing.

NA: And like calligraphy too. Calligraphy is a language that you are supposed to read yet cannot decode…

RH: … especially when you see it painted in continuous arabesques across walls, reams of writing translated into painting or relief sculpture, as you do in the Taj Mahal or in the Alhambra in Granada.

VM: Yes, in this sense, my painting of the walls of the 'Chamber' was like calligraphy. The sentence goes forward and cannot come back. It is not drafted or copied. It is spontaneous. As you say, Nancy, there is a script but it is not readable. It narrates something, it has characters and grammar, but it is not a simple narrative.

RH: And it expands into a choreography of dream and nightmare!

VM: You can say that. It's like this. Both of you know language so well and have such a large vocabulary. Sometimes, you would pick up a pad and start writing, and certain words flow by themselves, by free association. The pad is small, but your whole experience and perception and skill are going into your words. Certain words come automatically and what has happened with Ranjit as a poet and Nancy as a critic, all that will flow onto the paper. It is the same case with the painter. I experienced it, with the 'Chamber'.

I could draw and draw from my thoughts and my life's happenings, meters upon meters.

NA: Do you also think that the 'Chamber' is a breakthrough work at this stage of your career, because it gave you the freedom to liberate yourself from the content of the painting, however important that is, and to perform a far more private meditation on painterly language?

RH: While working on it, you developed a new form of painterly labour, a discipline of thinking and executing a mural-scale, room-shaped work across a set of individual panels. Panels that you would see fully assembled only during the exhibition.

NA: So the 'Chamber' was a new formal risk, a wager you made with curatorial desire and architectural circumstance!

VM: You know, my friends, one thing leads to another in life! Earlier, the content was very important, bearing witness to a specific situation, reacting drastically to a drastic condition that you have gone through. Then you become more settled in your mind, you move on, you become analytical and cool. You look beyond your own life story and examine the causes of the kind of turmoil you have suffered. The mind spreads its wings and moves around the globe and you adopt different people's reality. You see what is happening in Palestine, in Iraq, in Iran, in Afghanistan. Something changes in your practice too. Your hands move according to this new mental state.

When this connectivity happens between your situation and different global realities, you can react in many ways. You can adapt and adopt and become urbane and cosmopolitan. You may realise that other people have suffered the same wounds as you have, which you did not realise when you were hit hard by history and thought only you were hit that hard. But there is the danger that you can reject and withdraw, and become regimented and orthodox, fundamentalist. Everything depends on how you choose to respond to the new worlds that open in front of you.

Your wound may still be there, but you learn to go beyond it. With 'Shrapnel', both the exhibition and the continuing projects in video and animation, I am learning to draw on a larger conceptual space, make a more flexible language. I am trying to give more strength to the language than the content now, because, finally, the forefront of art practice is the language you develop. The content is the background. I do not want my content to be heavier than my language. You can have very politically correct content and your language can be all cliché.

NA: A lot of what passes for 'political art' is just an illustration of concepts or problems.

VM: That is because the content is so heavy and there is no new language. But it is easy for the public to grasp and the media to review. For a poet, his own special form of words is important, not that he is writing about love, war, dying and all the great themes. What have you expressed, how have you expressed it, how have you put yourself into these themes—that is important. I ask the same question as a painter: Where am I in what I have painted? My art may have a social or political statement, but it is art, it is not a platform to shout slogans or to let others know how committed you are to some cause.

NA: You are so right, Veer. Sometimes, you do not know whether to be amused or angry when you see young artists, who have not suffered any political crisis or historical tragedy in their own lives, who are not diasporic, just pick up information from the newspapers, images from television and the Internet, and package all this together. It has become a formula, they make pictures of events. That is the level to which the art that I once described as 'new mediatic realism' has declined. Today, people who repeat the formula come and tell me proudly that their art is 'new mediatic realism'. Can you believe it! 'Political art' of that kind is the most apolitical art there is!

VM: Exactly! I agree. 'Political art' of that kind is just trendy. You could call it fashion painting. Its content doesn't come from experience or serious concern. It comes from the media flow. If you have ever really experienced a political crisis or historical tragedy, as you are saying, you will try and create a language to translate the negative energy of sorrow and hurt into a more positive force. You will move beyond, and this will make you strong. Whereas, as you said, people today make pictures of events and call that a political painting.

Many times, they will not know the geography of Iran or where Baghdad is. But they take screen-grabs from CNN and BBC. I don't mean that artists or writers have necessarily to be part of a war, or that they can only express a response to a tragedy if they have been directly affected by it. But it is becoming more and more important to study events from the appropriate historical and cultural perspectives, and to see how these relate to your personal beliefs—rather than just making a work from a passing reference.

RH: This is a problem that Nancy and I have, when we look at so much that's going on in Indian art. Why does every new tendency in Indian art become a style? It starts as a genuine practice, responding to genuine historical or conceptual needs, but soon becomes a style adopted to signal membership of a club, to gain access to grants, or simply to sound sufficiently important. In different generations, this has happened with abstraction, political art, the installation, video, and the collective as a form. These things don't retain the vitality of choices made under particular circumstances.

NA: What began as a resistance to the mainstream becomes itself a part of the mainstream menu of options.

VM: Some artists think that video is not demanding, it is fashionable, and so they do it. But it also has a history, an academic basis, a context, which they do not always know. If you are training as a painter, it takes many years for your brush to gain maturity. The same is the case with video. You cannot just switch on the camera and start shooting, and think at the end you will have a video work you can show.

NA: Today, even an artist who has made an amateurish video thinks he or she is more cutting-edge than an artist who paints. Even if the work is half-baked, poor student work made in complete ignorance of the history of cinema, the history of video art, and the history of new media art. What is fashionable is seen as more important!

VM: I agree! And these false values seep into the new generation that is coming into the art schools. Many of them think: This is it, this is what we should be doing! And they repeat the half-baked ideas and produce bad work. But we also see some good video works around. One has to understand the depth of the medium, instead of getting carried away by a trend.

No medium is bad or outdated. Every medium can be practised in a way that suits the demands of your content and handling. And yes, you have to know the history of your medium. I can think of some very basic video works that have gained importance in our art world—they are like child's play when you look at video art being made in the advanced societies. Just because a medium is new here, we cannot excuse all the mistakes and stupidities made in its name! Whether it is painting or video or installation, you have to apply the same exacting standards. In India, the problem is that some of our artists operate from a Brahmin position. They think they are born to the privileges of being artists. They will do anything they like, and still think they have done a good *pooja* and written a great scripture, because they are Brahmins! They lay down the law on what is art and what is not art, because they are Brahmins, and people follow them.

NA: In the art world, as in every other sector of Indian society, we confront the persistence of caste.

VM: If we had a situation where different kinds of art practitioners had their different myths and theories and histories and approaches, we would have come to the forefront as a rich visual arts culture in the world. Instead, we are trying to follow what we think is the history of global art, and our train always reaches every station a decade late.

NA: There is a strong strain of fixated and dogmatic thinking in our cultural sphere. Maybe we need to get off this train and find a new track! Also, any form of resistance in terms of medium, content or whatever else, always gets co-opted by the establishment. It is almost immediately regimentalised and institutionalised by the market, by the academy that is working with the market, by the approval of collectors and, until the recession, of investors. Protest doesn't remain a protest. We are so easily co-opted.

RH: The reflexes of caste society predispose Indians towards a defensive withholding of information, and against generosity and sharing. The desire is not to have freedom, but to have power. Not the liberty to explore, but the hunger for control.

NA: And to achieve an aspirational status.

RH: Yes. And the idea, the concept is emphasised over any hands-on execution. That also marks the persistence of Brahmanical thinking.

VM: You won't get down and work with your hands and develop a technology that reflects original thought.

RH: You have a great idea and then you hire assistants to execute it. Of course, if you're working on sculpture, large-scale painting or technology-based art, you have to distribute and delegate your process. But I have seen artists use the same logic, when their practice does not require it. So, ultimately, you do less and less yourself, you grow more and more distant from what you make—or what is being made in your name and under your signature—and the less and less effective your art is.

VM: Definitely.

NA: It is a remote art, made by giving instructions on a mobile.

VM: Yes, it is a different way of making art. There is nothing wrong with having assistants for some sorts and scales of art-making, as you say. There is nothing wrong with that practice in itself. The question is: How closely is one involved with the act of making, emotionally and otherwise? Sometimes, yes, art becomes a product associated with a brand name. Market pressures also play their role, just the pressure to appear 'contemporary' does. Some artists try to look trendy by mixing media without thinking out a proper logic. We look at what others are doing, and do the same. When, in fact, we should move fast and make our own niche, speaking from our part of the world. We have so much potential, diversity, and richness here, from which we can create so many new forms. But the Brahmins won't let you do it. They will make you follow the trends.

NA: To paraphrase it, our art is never free of fear. We always fear freedom somehow and we prefer regimentation. We feel very comfortable being our little selves, following the wind and the tide of what is widely accepted to be the new, never making the new. Wherever the tide shifts, we shift in the same direction.

VM: There is also the factor of the economy. The norm is: What sells is art. And this norm infects the next generation. Sometimes, it is the sale value rather than the strength of the art that dictates belief in that art. I see this kind of belief taking over in the academic institutions. I went once to Santiniketan as an examiner, and felt so disturbed to see the copies of copies that students were making, because they thought such and such an artist was a trend-leader, was selling well. What does this lead to? Earlier, students followed their teachers, followed the visionary masters. Today, they follow the market.

It is true that the boom gave us a scale, which I, as an artist, appreciate. We started working on large and more exciting projects that had not been possible without money, and we received many advantages. But the boom also produced too many market images! Art is now a respectable profession. Parents encourage their children to join art school—unlike in the past, when it was like committing suicide to go to art school, defying social norms and embracing insecurity. *Junoon*, passion, was the driving force. And yet I appreciate the many young talents that are emerging with new ideas and experiments. Technology has added a new dimension to their work, and a number of them are making their mark on the global scene.

RH: But we need an ethic to go with the augmented scale and the advantages that the boom has generated.

VM: Yes. That is important. Artists should always look back and ask themselves, 'Why did we come into art?'

NA: Veer, thank you so much for a truly rich conversation.

Authors' Biography

RANJIT HOSKOTE (born 1969) is a poet, cultural theorist and curator. He is the author of 19 books. These include five collections of poetry, most recently, *Vanishing Acts: New & Selected Poems 1985–2005* (New Delhi: Penguin, 2006) and *Die Ankunft der Vögel* (München: Carl Hanser Verlag, 2006). Hoskote has authored eight monographs, including *Bharti Kher* (New York: Jack Shainman Gallery, 2007); *The Crafting of Reality: Sudhir Patwardhan, Drawings* (Mumbai: foundation b & g, 2010); and *Zinny & Maidagan: Compartment/Das Abteil* (Frankfurt & Köln: Museum für Moderne Kunst/MMK & Verlag der Buchhandlung Walther König, 2010). He has collaborated on an artist book with Atul Dodiya, *Pale Ancestors* (Mumbai: Bodhi Art, 2008) and co-authored, with Ilija Trojanow, a history of cultural confluence, *Kampfabsage* (München: Random House/Blessing Verlag, 2007). Hoskote's essays have appeared in numerous international anthologies, including *Kapital und Karma* (eds. Gerald Matt, Angelika Fitz and Michael Wörgötter; Vienna & Ostfildern-Ruit: Kunsthalle Wien & Hatje Cantz, 2002); *The Making of Global City Regions* (ed. Klaus Segbers; Baltimore: Johns Hopkins University Press, 2007); *Art Basel Miami Transcripts* (ed. Hans Ulrich Obrist; Ostfildern-Ruit: Hatje Cantz, 2008); and *The Biennial Reader* (eds. Elena Filipovic, Marieke van Hal and Solveig Ovstebo; Ostfildern-Ruit: Hatje Cantz, 2010).

Hoskote has curated 20 exhibitions of Indian and international art, including a mid-career survey of Atul Dodiya (Japan Foundation, Tokyo, 2001) and a retrospective of Jehangir Sabavala (National Gallery of Modern Art, New Delhi and Mumbai,

2005–2006). He co-curated the trans-Asian collaborative project, 'Under Construction' (Japan Foundation, 2000–2002). Hoskote and Hyunjin Kim co-curated, with Artistic Director Okwui Enwezor, the 7th Gwangju Biennale (Korea, 2008). He has been writer-in-residence at the International Writing Program, University of Iowa (1995), Villa Waldberta, München (2003), Theater der Welt, Essen/ Mülheim (2010) and 'The Promised City' project, Berlin (2010). Hoskote is curatorial director, foundation b & g, Mumbai.

NANCY ADAJANIA (born 1971) is a cultural theorist, art critic, and independent curator. She has written and lectured extensively on extended sculpture, new media and public art at numerous international venues, including Documenta 11, Kassel; Zentrum für Kunst und Medientechnologie/ZKM, Karlsruhe; Neuer Berliner Kunstverein, Berlin; Künstlerhaus Wien, Vienna; the Gulbenkian Foundation, Lisbon; The Danish Contemporary Art Foundation, Copenhagen; and the Soma Museum, Seoul. Adajania was editor-in-chief of *Art India* (2000–2003), in which role she focused on creating contexts for public art, new media, and the relationship between the visual arts and political intervention. She has proposed several new theoretical models, including 'a new mediatic realism' (tracking the effects of mediatic reality on painting); 'new-context media' (mapping the postcolonial location of video and net-based practices); 'Aladdin's cave, a new urban sociology of self-representation' (accounting for the politicisation of visual culture), and 'televisual assemblies' (tracing the illusion of democratic performativity produced by contemporary mass media, by contrast with what she terms a 'performative democracy' anchored in a discourse of rights and entitlements).

Adajania has curated 'Avatars of the Object: Sculptural Projections' (NCPA/Guild Art Gallery, Mumbai, 2006) and 'The Landscapes of Where' (Galerie Mirchandani + Steinruecke, Mumbai, 2009). She co-curated 'Zoom: Art in Contemporary India' (Culturgest Museum, Lisbon, 2004). Adajania has written numerous catalogue essays on established and emerging artists, including K. G. Subramanyan, Atul Dodiya, Nalini Malani, Vivan Sundaram, Navjot, Anju Dodiya, Gargi Raina, Shilpa Gupta, Anant Joshi, Mithu Sen, Ashim Purkayastha, Ashok Sukumaran, T. V. Santhosh, Reena Saini Kallat, Prajakta Palav, Prajakta Potnis, and Gigi Scaria, among others. Adajania is the editor of *Shilpa Gupta* (München/New York: Prestel, 2010). Adajania has been an associate fellow of Sarai-Centre for the Study of Developing Societies, New Delhi, and is currently research scholar-in-residence at BAK/basis voor aktuele kunst, Utrecht (2010–2011).